Psychic Development

The Ultimate Beginner's Guide to developing psychic abilities, clairvoyance, and third eye awakening

Table of Contents

Introduction

Thank you for taking the time to read this book on psychic development.

This book covers the topic of psychic development and will educate you on the many different psychic abilities that people can possess. Everyone is born with psychic abilities, but unfortunately most never tap in to and develop these hidden skills.

Over the following chapters, you will learn about the many different psychic abilities that exist, as well as how to develop them further through meditation, chakra balancing, and dedicated activities designed specifically for each psychic skill that you wish to enhance. In addition, you will also learn about spirit guides and how you can communicate with them in order to improve your abilities and live a more fulfilled life.

At the completion of this book you will have a good understanding of the many different psychic skills, and be armed with a range of strategies and activities that will help you to further develop these abilities!

Once again, thanks for choosing this book, I hope you find it to be helpful!

Chapter 1 – The Different Types of Psychic Abilities

While all people possess some psychic ability, there are those to who these skills come naturally. Also commonly referred to as "sensitives", these people are gifted with remarkable abilities that allow them to read and understand certain matters that defy science and rationality.

Some people are born with a higher level of perception than most. Some, however, have only unlocked these skills later on after being triggered by serendipitous but typically unfortunate moments in life. There are also people who recognized their psychic potential, and from there on, decided to pursue the development of their metaphysical attributes. Whatever the origin of these unexplainable skills may be, it is important first to learn about the various types of psychic abilities that humans may possess.

1. Aura Reading

Aura readers are individuals who can perceive the layers of colorful energy fields that surround another living being. An aura is a widely recognized phenomenon among spiritual experts and, interpreting the colors it exhibits can reveal a lot of personal information. This includes but is not limited to emotions, personality traits, career preferences, ideal romantic partners, and financial status.

2. Channeling

To channel a spirit, a psychic uses their ability to become a bridge between the physical and spiritual worlds. More commonly referred to as "mediums," these people facilitate communication between the living, and other entities that belong in other dimensions.

The intensity of the manifestation of this ability varies depending on the level of spirituality of the person, and the strength of the entity that is trying to communicate. In some extreme cases, a medium may allow a spirit to take full control of their body in order to better relay the message the spirit wants to convey. More often, however, the ability is limited only to specific means of communication, such as oral or written communication.

3. Clairaudience

This ability allows a person to harness various types of energies in order to listen in on certain events that occur outside the range of normal human hearing capacity. Some are so adept at being clairaudient that they can hear an incident happening from across the world.

Furthermore, there are also psychics with this ability who are able to hear matters that take place outside the known world. According to parapsychology experts, sounds originating from the spirit world usually take a musical form. Even inanimate objects emit sounds that can be perceived by clairaudients. This is more commonly observed among artifacts and crystals.

4. Clairgustance and Clairsalience

These abilities are usually linked with one another since our sense of taste and smell are similarly connected as well. People who can perceive psychic information through a smell that did not originate from any physical source are said to be in possession of the skill called clairsalience. On the other hand, tasting something without any foreign stimuli present on your tongue indicates that you are capable of clairgustance.

Further interpretations of this psychic information can be made through the use of intuition and analysis. For example, tasting blood in your mouth and smelling it in the air may indicate a looming violent death or accident.

5. Claircognizance

Also known as clear recognition or knowing, this ability allows the person to gain information on matters that he or she does not have prior knowledge about. The psychic will not be able to explain this in terms of objective terms, but they will be certain that the information is accurate.

Some experts believe that this is actually a form of channeling, wherein the information is passed on by the person's spirit guide or even their own higher self. However, there is no hard evidence of such theory, so this ability remains to be an area of wide speculation among parapsychologists.

6. Clairsentience

Clairsentient individuals can feel the different forms of energies that surround them or other people. As they continue to train their abilities, they can eventually be able to increase their sensitivity to the point that they can sense any and all types of energies around them.

7. Clairvoyance

Clairvoyant people are gifted with special sight that permits them to see beyond what the eyes can sense. The scope of this skill can range from seeing alternate realities that differ from the physical world, to simply seeing the auras and energies that surround other people.

8. Divination

This is the practice of answering questions by observing the signs that naturally occur within the psychic's environment, and by communicating with spirits from different dimensions. Various methods of divination have been developed and passed on to other practitioners over the years. Typically, these methods require certain tools to increase the success rate of their attempts to communicate with spirits. Commonly used objects for divination include the following:

- o Crystal Balls

- o Ouija Boards

- o   Tarot Cards

- o   Pendulums

- o   Tea Leaves

9. Intuition

By strengthening their wills, intuitive people can learn and understand someone or something on a deeper and more detailed level without going through the regular thought process that other normal humans follow. These people have a high level of intuition.

In some cases, the speed of their realizations and comprehension are viewed as a matter of instinct or high intelligence. However, depending on the situation wherein this ability has been exhibited by a psychic person, intuition can be an unexplainable phenomenon that challenges those who want to view this skill from an objective lens.

10. Lucid Dreaming

If a person can control their dreams to either a limited or full extent, then they would be considered as a lucid dreamer in psychic terms. Achieving the full potential of this skill induces another type of psychic ability—lucid projection or more commonly known as astral traveling.

11. Lucid Projection (Astral Travel)

A high level of lucidity while asleep can bring about the ability to leave behind the physical body in order to explore realms outside the known world. When this happens, the person takes full control of their consciousness and becomes an astral traveler. During this period, their awareness of both physical and non-physical matters heightens to a great degree, enabling them to gather information that simply cannot be attainable when awake.

12. Precognition

People who can look into the future and see the possible realities that may take place are believed to have the skill of precognition. This usually appears in the form of visions depicting moments that have yet to happen in the current timeline. Others describe it as having a feeling that something significant is about to happen, be it good or bad.

However, since humans can still exercise their free will, there is no assurance that such readings of the future will come to pass. There may be other choices that a person may take to alter the future, hence the pervasive disbelief over this ability among those who do not have a full grasp of its true nature.

13. Psychic Healing

There are two key requirements in order to become a psychic healer. First, the person must be so well attuned with their personal spirituality that they can bring forth key information from non-physical dimensions into the physical reality. Such specialized knowledge is typically transmitted through telepathy. Psychics describe this experience as having thoughts or feelings that are completely separate from their own.

Second, there must be a large amount of ectoplasmic energy surrounding the person. Having access to this will allow a body part of the given person—usually a hand or two—to dematerialize and rematerialize at will. This allows the psychic healer to perform operations without having to undergo normal procedures followed by actual medical professionals.

The medical capabilities of psychic healers are not honed through years of education and practice. Rather, they are able to perform such acts through the guidance of non-physical entities. Though not commonly found in Western countries, there are plenty of stories about the controversial feats of psychic healers in Asia, particularly in China and the Philippines.

14. Psychography

Also referred to as automatic writing, this skill enables a person to connect the physical and non-physical worlds by relaying messages from the latter in written form. The psychics themselves have no control whatsoever about the content of the message. They only write down what is dictated to them usually through intrusive thoughts or even spoken words that only they can hear. During the course of this interaction, the non-physical entities use the psychics as instruments in order to reach out to the known world for whatever reason has caused them to do so.

15. Psychometry

This skill is frequently featured in films and television show whenever a psychic has been asked to come in and assist with the search of a missing person. The psychic touches an object that belonged to the missing person in order to gain information and insights about the given case. This is made possible by sensing and interpreting the different energies from the owner that remain stuck in the object.

In other instances, psychometrists use their skills to simply get a reading of a certain individual's personality. Others take this further by uncovering the past lives of the owner of the object.

16. Psychophony

Psychophony bears striking similarities with psychography, except for one element. Instead of writing down information from beyond our world, a psychophonist will transmit messages through the spoken word. They do not have control over what will be said nor the manner of speaking. Essentially, non-physical entities are using these psychics as their mouthpiece in order to manifest here in the physical world.

17. Remote-Viewing

This skill refers to the gift possessed by people who can clearly see events, people, or places that are located far from them. They can also see into the non-physical realm without having to go to sleep like those who are capable of lucid projection. Unlike lucid dreamers, remote viewers have the ability to describe what is happening in real-time, even without closing their eyes to concentrate on the images they are seeing.

18. Retrocognition

Acquiring information about the past—whether from a person's current life or past lives—comprises the psychic abilities of a retrocognitor. The time spent by the consciousness in between two lives is also accessible for those who possess this skill. Knowledge of such experiences may be a useful resource for understanding someone's motives and decisions, especially when that individual isn't forthcoming with such personal details.

19. Telekinesis

Psychics who can move objects without having to touch them are exhibiting telekinesis. In some cases, the psychic can also make something disappear and reappear, while others can utilize this power to search for a missing object.

20. Telepathy

Information transmitted from one mind to another can be read by a telepath. Experts in parapsychology suggest that every human is a telepath by nature. The sensitivity level of the consciousness, however, determines if the message will be recognized and interpreted according to how the sender originally intended it to be.

Even after several years of research in the spiritual arts, there is still no definitive evidence that proves or disproves the authenticity of psychic abilities. Scientists continue to refute claims from psychics since most of these reports are not solid and could not somehow be replicated under controlled circumstances. However, witnesses of psychic phenomena still attest to what they have seen and experienced.

There is also the existence of frauds who only mimic what real psychics can do for their own financial gain. Some genuine psychics also feel the need to avoid the spotlight for various personal reasons, choosing only to use their abilities to quietly help other people by using their special gifts. Even more unfortunate are those people who try to suppress their psychic abilities due to fear, or in order to conform to their community's view of spirituality.

Learning and understanding your psychic abilities is the healthy way of removing the stigma and apprehensions since what we do not know often inspires fear within us. These abilities are not inherently good or bad; the way you harness them will define how you will be regarded by other people and spiritual entities.

Chapter 2 – How to Develop Your Psychic Abilities

Most people have asked this question at some point in their lives: Am I psychic? Perhaps there was one instance wherein you guessed correctly how a certain matter would be resolved. Or maybe you once had an out-of-body experience that you simply cannot describe completely in words. The answer is simpler than you think.

Every human is psychic.

However, not everyone is on the same level. When it comes to psychic abilities, the difference between one person and another lies in the effort exerted in developing said abilities to their fullest capacity. We all possess these innate abilities, but only few people are willing to undergo years of training and learning all the right techniques that can get them to the next level.

Psychic abilities are similar to any other skill that a person may possess. Much like when you are learning to play the piano, a high motivation to learn and an unwavering dedication to the craft is the key to mastery of these abilities.

It is important, however, to always remember that some people are born with a greater talent for a specific ability than others. In such cases, harnessing these gifts is just a natural part of their lives. For the other people without these innate talents, they will likely want to learn more about the different skills in order to further improve or increase their control over them.

Physical Perception vs. Psychic Perception

In order to understand how a psychic ability manifests in real life, you have to learn first how humans process information through their consciousness. Touching a bowl right out of the microwave will tell you that the object is hot. You know this through your physical sense of touch. On the other hand, a persistent, tingling sensation on your forehead while lying alone in bed can signify a psychic experience. If you have determined that no object or living being inside the room could have touched your forehead, then you are likely perceiving this sensation through your energy body.

When you fix your gaze on someone and take note of the details of his facial features and the clothes he is wearing, you are receiving information from your eyes. However, if you suddenly notice a layer of light surrounding this person, then you might be seeing his aura through your psychic sight. To differentiate this from lights that emanate from a physical light source, check if the layer of light bears different colors, which move and change along with the person himself. If it does, then you are seeing something that should be readily seen by the naked eye since auras are basically electromagnetic fields that envelop our bodies as a reflection of our current moods and personalities.

Some people may disregard such experiences as mere by-products of an overactive imagination. However, the obvious difference lies in the amount of control you have over your perceptions. When you imagine something, you decide what is going to be in there. On the other hand, psychic experiences are rarely, if ever, within the control of an individual. In fact, the more passive you are, the more likely you are to receive psychic information than when you try to force such experiences to happen. Given these facts, learning how to correctly identify the cause of a stimulus is a vital skill in developing your psychic abilities.

Awakening Your Psychic Abilities

Abilities that are tied with our spirituality are naturally occurring among humans. However, there are certain skills that are innately present, while others can be learned. Therefore, a person may be talented at telekinesis, but relatively inexperienced when it comes to retrocognition.

According to experts, there is no single standard way to awaken our psychic abilities. Everybody's experience is unique to their own, and therefore, the results of going through such remarkable events will vary depending on the person. In a survey conducted among psychics, here is a list of the most common trigger points that helped to activate or further develop their special abilities:

- **Near-Death Experience or Accident**

  Sometimes, when a person has an uncomfortably close encounter with death, they will soon begin experiencing unexplainable psychic episodes. In other cases, people who have nearly died have reported seeing spirits after they recovered from their harrowing experience. Well-known examples of psychics who have started this way are Maureen Hancock, Doreen Virtue, and John Holland.

- **Death of a Loved One**

  After losing a loved one, some people turn to their spirituality in order to relieve them from their grief. Even if the person was not normally in touch with this aspect of their life beforehand, the increased focus on the soul and energies can bring about a psychic awakening.

- **Childbirth**

  Many people believe that a mother's intuition is always right. According to some experts, this belief originates from the time a woman gives birth to her child. During this moment, the new parents, particular the mother, experience a spike in the level of intuition as a response to the welcomed addition to their family. This heightened intuition can further lead on to the development of other psychic abilities that have not been activated yet.

- **Chakra Healing**

  In some cases, the act of cleaning away the negativities and blockages from the chakra can awaken a person's psychic abilities by mere happenstance. This occurs because during healing sessions, the vibrations within the said person increase, as well as the flow rate of energy to the body. These sudden changes can transform one's consciousness, as a side-effect.

Ten Signs of a Psychic Awakening

A psychic awakening often happens when a person is subjected to life-altering events, which then opens up their spirits to new experiences and psychic energies. You can determine for yourself if your special abilities have been activated through the following signs:

1. **Presence of a Tingling Sensation**

    When a chakra has been opened up, you may start feeling a tingling sensation or pressure in specific points in your body. When it comes to psychic abilities, these new sensations are typically felt near the forehead or at the top of the head. During the initial stages, people report that the tingling feeling is too strong to be ignored, but it eventually wanes down to manageable levels as your body becomes accustomed to the new energies that are being received.

2. **Stronger Spiritual Connection**

    When you have activated your psychic abilities, you will begin to notice more and more the various spirits that inhabit this world. This due to your growing connection with the spiritual world. For some people, awakening their psychic abilities has led them to gain the capacity to converse with the departed souls of their loved ones, and even those of other people. On the other hand, for the majority of those with newly awakened psychic abilities, the increased connection with spirits allows them to interact with their spirit guides more frequently and more effectively.

3. Desire to Stay Away from Negativity

Being more sensitive about the feelings of other people is another sign that you should be looking out for. Due to this heightened sensitivity, you will begin feeling physically and emotionally drained after being exposed to dramatic or stressful people. Respect yourself and the privacy of others by choosing to stay away from situations that would only breed negativity.

4. Preference for Healthier Foods

As a result of increased vibrations in your body brought about by your newly activated psychic abilities, you might find yourself craving for healthier alternatives to your regular diet. This is a natural reaction by your body, which is instinctively seeking for nourishment that would satisfy your unconscious need for a higher rate of vibrations within your body.

5. Desire to Learn More About Your Spiritual Side

People who have recently opened themselves up to the spirit world and other non-physical dimensions will develop an appetite for any bit of knowledge they can get their hands on about this new aspect of their lives. They will actively look for books to read and find ways to practice their psychic abilities. Since they are now following the spiritual path of their existence, it is only natural for humans to be curious about what lies ahead of them.

6. Vivid Dreams

Having more frequent dreams that feature vivid details is indicative of an awakening within your spirit. This observed phenomenon happens for two reasons. First, there is less resistance in your physical, mental, and spiritual boundaries when you are asleep. The brain is not trying to process every stimulus it receives, and therefore more information gets through into your consciousness. For example, during the day when you are awake, you might convince yourself that an unlikely incident happened as a result of mere coincidence, when really it occurred because of spiritual intervention. However, when you are asleep, the barriers go down, thereby making you more receptive towards energies and signals that originated from outside this world.

The second reason is that as you become more in touch with your spiritual side, the easier it becomes for you to reach deeper levels of your consciousness, which includes the dream state. You will gradually get a better grasp of your new skills, and then you will be able to further explore the various non-physical dimensions that have opened up to you.

7. Increased Sensitivity of Your Physical Senses

Heightened senses are one of the most definite signs that something has changed within your body. If you can suddenly see sparks and twinkling lights from the corner of your eye, or if you can somehow hear someone speaking from a range that should not be normally possible, then you have awakened your psychic senses. Known also as the "clairs", these senses are characterized by an increased capacity to receive and process psychic information through the various sense organs.

8. More Accurate Intuition

Some people find it exciting—others find it frightening—to have the ability to sense what is about to happen. This can take many forms, including but not limited to intrusive thoughts and visions.

If you belong to the group of people who are afraid of their new skills and what they will change in their lives, there are various ways to control your gifts so that they will not be activated at all times. Practice these methods so that you can fully embrace this new side of your being.

9. Headaches

Throbbing pains in the head are often caused by the sudden influx of energy into our system. A way to alleviate this inconvenience is by soaking both feet in warm water. The temperature of the water can help bring down the energy to your lower limbs, away from the top of your head where it has accumulated.

Adding essential oils and Epsom salts can further increase the effectivity of the foot soak. However, it is still advisable to consult your doctor as well, just so you can rule out any other possible medical cause of your headache.

10. Changing Friends

A psychic awakening can bring about a lot of new things into your life, and as a result, you might find yourself outgrowing some of your existing friends. This may be caused by your new ability to better assess and understand your compatibility with them in terms of spirituality and emotional stability. Or perhaps, it may be due to your new focus in life, which unfortunately has caused them to fall by the wayside. Such partings are expected, but do not worry because you will come across new people who will gladly join you in your quest for the mastery of your psychic abilities.

At the beginning, it is alright to feel apprehensive about the many changes that are occurring in your life due to your psychic awakening. Something has shifted within you as well, and you can now regard yourself as an intuitive being who is connected closely with your spirituality. Plenty of other people feel the same way as you do, so it might be helpful to seek them out and open up about doubts and questions in order to attain peace of mind, and fully embrace your newfound psychic abilities.

Exercising Your Psychic Abilities

In order to fully assess your current capabilities, you have to learn how to work and channel energies into your chakras. Furthermore, you have to be courageous in attempting new ways to improve your perceptive skills in order to ensure a steady development of your psychic abilities.

There are two approaches that psychics commonly practice to develop their abilities. Each one has their own advantages and disadvantages, but it is up to decide which of the two will better fit your objectives and current lifestyle. You may also have the option of combining the two methods by balancing the extent of their applications to your life:

1. **Structured Attempts**

    This method requires you to devote at least one hour per day to practicing your skills in the ideal condition and environment that would best draw out your full capacity. During this time, your attention should be focused only on learning new theories and trying out techniques related to the psychic ability that you want to develop.

    For example, let's imagine that you are trying to improve your control over your clairvoyance or psychic sight. Upon assessing your pending chores and prior commitments, you have decided to conduct your practice session on a Sunday afternoon since there are fewer interruptions during that time of the day. Some people, however, prefer doing this exercise at three in the morning, when everyone else is sound asleep. However, this would require you to go to sleep early in order to let your body rest well before the upcoming strenuous activity. The important thing is simply to choose the best time for yourself, when your mind will be clear and free of distractions.

The day before your scheduled session, you should advise your family and friends that you need some alone time. Also, it's a good idea to turn off your phone just so you can fully disconnect from the outside world. Once you are locked inside your solitude space, you can now proceed with your structured attempt to control your clairvoyance.

Parapsychologists recommend using pillows to elevate your head and upper body in a 30-degree angle. This position will allow you to comfortably view your toes without having to lean forward. While lying down, close your eyes and try to focus on the energy you feel in your body for about 15 minutes. This will bring your entire body into a relaxed state that will then allow your consciousness to take over.

After some time has elapsed, open your eyes and focus on observing your own aura by inspecting your toes for the presence of a surrounding energy field. Keep an eye out as well for any movement or disruptions within your peripheral vision. Continue doing these activities for the next 30 minutes.

During the last 15 minutes of your session, write down in a journal the perceptions you have made during the course of the exercise. Take note as well the points that worked well for you, and the ones that did not go so well. If possible, try to identify the probable causes for such hindrances so that you can refer back to this information later on.

2. Incorporated into a Daily Routine

There are various points throughout the day where we can incorporate psychic exercises without taking up much effort and time. For instance, when the internet connection is acting up, but you want to browse for something to buy on a website, you will likely space out while waiting for the page to load. Instead of just waiting for the images to come up, try to access your chakras and check if they are currently active or if they are in need of a cleanup.

An extended meeting where your full attention is not required can be an excellent way of practicing your psychic senses. Feel the energy flowing around the room and see if you can distinguish the different energies from each other.

There are people who cannot fathom how this could be worked into their daily routine mainly because they segregate their spiritual interests from the other aspects of their lives. As a result, they tend to repress the urge to learn and practice, and ignore the different opportunities presented to them. Others feel the need to hide away their psychic abilities from other people in fear of being judged or mocked for their beliefs.

Your psychic development should not be hampered down by these self-imposed restrictions and limitations. There are vast unexplored dimensions that you can unlock for yourself if you are simply willing to try. By doing so, you will gain experiences that would not have had happened to you if you had chosen to remain within your comfort zone.

The two approaches differ greatly from one another, but both can be helpful in developing your psychic abilities. Structured attempts are vital in gaining a deeper understanding of your skills, while squeezing your exercises in between daily tasks can let you have a richer, more practical view of what you are capable of doing.

Regardless of which method you choose for yourself, the primary goal should be to make your psychic abilities become part of your "second nature." This means that even if you are not actively exerting effort to use them, you can wield your abilities when you do need them.

Maintaining a high level of interest in your spirituality is important in the overall success of your exercises. Without this, your efforts will quickly turn into heavy obligations that you will dread doing.

Chapter 3 – Awakening and Developing Your Third Eye

The third eye has long been revered as a spiritual symbol by different cultures and religions across the world. In general, it is considered as a representation of a person's ability to overcome various challenges that may be encountered throughout their life. The beliefs surrounding the third eye, however, vary according to the pervading traditional practices of the area. For example, Eastern cultures believe that the third eye has a physical component that can be awakened through meditation and concentration efforts.

Others regard the third eye in a more metaphysical sense, wherein it serves as a window to a person's consciousness and enlightened mind. An individual with an awakened third eye has the ability to perceive the world in an entirely different light. The psychic abilities possessed by said person become more enhanced as well, allowing them to achieve greater things using their spiritual gifts.

In terms of the chakras—or the centers of energy within the body as identified first by the Indians—the third eye is known as the Ajna chakra. It is physically located in the middle of the eyebrows and is believed to be the gateway to the divine dimensions.

People who have managed to open and achieve balance in this chakra are said to develop keen insights about the world surrounding them. They also become more open-minded about intellectual matters as they gain better connections with their intuition and rationality. Due to these benefits, many people aim to awaken their third eyes and further develop into better versions of themselves, especially in relation to their spiritual fulfillment.

Awakening the Third Eye

A wholehearted commitment to improving your spirituality is the key to opening the third eye. It is important to note that this will not happen overnight. However, if you know which methods can hasten the process, then small changes in your personal life and abilities can be observed day by day.

Most people recognize that there are three main stages of awakening. A person must go through each of the steps listed in each stage so as to achieve the desired results. There are shortcuts that may be taken, but by doing so, you are compromising the chances of realizing the full potential of your third eye.

- **Crystals and Precious Stones**

  Parapsychologists recommend the usage of crystals and gemstones for channeling the right type of energies and spirits that you are seeking. Since the ajna chakra is associated with purple, you may consider purchasing pieces of jewelry that feature crystals and precious stones within that range of color.

  Having wearable accessories that incorporate crystals will allow you to bring them with you wherever you go, unlike with large pieces that may only be displayed as a décor in your house or workspace. Some people do prefer larger stones which they carry around in their pockets or enclosed in the palms of their hands. Whatever type you choose, it is important to keep the purple crystals or gemstone close to you.

There is a wide range of selection available for those who are pursuing the opening of their third eye. Most experts suggest classic options such as amethyst, sodalite, tourmaline, and rhodonite. Others pick purple variations of sapphire or fluorite to sharpen their intuition and achieve clarity in their minds. Once you have selected and bought your crystals and precious stones, you are now more equipped for the next step of awakening your third eye.

- **Meditation**

During the initial series of meditation, your first objective should be to simply locate the third eye. There are seven chakras in the human body. Tapping into each them will bring forth different effects to your physical and mental health. Identifying where the ajna chakra is will allow you to focus your mind onto opening the third eye. For your guidance, concentrate on the upper frontal portion of your head. Imagine a circle forming in between your eyebrows until you can sense your mind opening up to the sensation.

Using a purple crystal or gemstone can also help you to locate your third eye during meditation. You may either squeeze the object inside the palm of your hand, or press the crystal or stone against your forehead, ideally near or exactly on the probable location of the third eye. This will keep you focused on your objective, as well as lessen the possibility of being distracted by other external factors.

Meditation is best done in a place that you find as comfortable as possible. Achieving mental clarity requires an immense amount of effort, so it is advisable to stay away from any possible sources of distraction. Some people choose a quiet room where they can be totally alone with their thoughts. Others opt to be out in nature, where soothing sounds can take them deeper into their meditation. Whatever your preference is, make sure that you choose a place where you can relax both your body and mind.

Correcting your posture and sitting comfortably can further improve your chances of opening the third eye through meditation. Here are some of the common methods employed by meditation experts to become more comfortable and be more focused during their meditation:

- o If you spend the majority of the day sitting down, try to make time for you to practice sitting directly on the ground. This will allow your body to acclimate to the sitting positions used when meditating.

- o More people prefer sitting down on the ground with crossed legs compared to those who rest their hips on the backsides of their folded legs. However, try both and see which position is most comfortable for you.

- o Seat cushions may be used if you simply cannot find a comfortable spot while in a sitting position.

- o If sitting is not really an option for you, then you may go for walking meditation. However, it is important to first plan ahead the path that you will take during this activity. There must be no distractions at all in order to fully immerse yourself in the meditation.

Other than cushions, certain objects may help you achieve the right level of comfort for meditation. For example, candles are considered to be excellent focal objects since the flickering of the flame is simple enough for the eyes to follow without disrupting your concentration.

Some people, however, choose to imagine different sceneries instead. As an example, they may try to conjure up an image of beautiful flowers, or the calming vista of being atop a mountain after a long hike.

Another recommended technique is picking a mantra—a word or a phrase that you will repeat throughout the meditation process. It may be spoken out under your breath or just whispered inside your head. For more effective mantras, choose something that has a special meaning to you. This allows the word or phrase to become more integrated into your consciousness. Since you are trying to open your third eye, you may opt to say something like "wisdom" or "clarity" in order to get your mind into the right space.

Meditation is not a one-time activity only. You may find yourself being distracted often during your first few tries. That is all right. Practice meditation until you find the right combination of positions and techniques that let you focus on your objective. Daily meditation can start with quick sessions of no more than five minutes. However, by gradually incorporating this into your daily routines, you will soon master this skill and be one step closer to opening your third eye.

- **Mindfulness**

A person with a high level of mindfulness can sense the various energies surrounding them on a deeper level. They are not only attuned with physical sensations, however. They can reach in deep within themselves to fully connect with the emotions they're feeling inside. For example, when a person is feeling stressed out after a long day at work, mindfulness can be exhibited by simply acknowledging their feelings rather than trying to deny or make up excuses for the negative energy around them.

To develop the capacity to recognize how the world, in general, affects you, it's recommended to go outside to explore your actual environment. Observe other people; Take note of the rustling leaves as the wind blowing past them. Appreciate the different shades of blue in the sky. Focus more on the outside world by leaving back at home any source of potential distractions like your cellphone or headphones.

Tapping into your creative side can also increase your mindfulness. Creating a piece of artwork or composing music can be meditative and may open up your mind to reaching new aspects of your spiritual side.

As you go through your everyday life, pay attention even to the tiniest things that form your daily routine. Feel how warm the water is while you are in the shower. Take a whiff of your freshly brewed coffee. Savor the buttery goodness of a croissant. Focusing on small things can slow down your pace and make you feel calmer even on the most hectic of days. By doing so, you may gradually find yourself accessing the third eye without even trying to do so directly.

Signs of a Successful Awakening

Once you have gone through the three stages of awakening the third eye, you will start feeling certain changes within your body. Here are two definitive signs indicating that you have been successful in achieving your objective:

- **Building Pressure in the Lower Middle Portion of the Forehead**

  The primary physical manifestation of an open third eye is signaled by a slight pressure in between the eyebrows, as if someone is touching you on that spot with their forefinger. Eventually, this sensation will spread throughout the adjacent areas, but the pressure will remain centralized in the middle of your eyebrows.

- **Appearance of Lights and Circular Shapes**

The most striking sign of an awakened third eye is the sudden appearance of lights inside your mind while deep in meditation or while you are using your third eye. At first, the lights may take on vague circular shapes, making them appear like simple white spots. As you go deeper into your meditation, those circles may begin to take another form as a white star with five points.

In some cases, these stars are also surrounded by a halo of gold and a dark blue background. Some people believe that this is the true and final form that symbolizes the third eye. Even more so, the same symbol can be found in different cultures and religious artworks around the world, proving that the form is universally recognized by people who have achieved mental and spiritual enlightenment.

Benefits of Awakening the Third Eye

When you have opened your third eye, you may expect gradual but persistent changes in your body and your personal interactions with the rest of the world. The benefits will become more pronounced as time goes on, and you will experience how such changes can affect your innate psychic abilities, particularly intuition. Your self-awareness will also improve, which makes you appreciate your gifts and quirks even more.

Having an open mind helps you to absorb more information about important matters that you used to ignore or overlook. Therefore, awakening the third eye can let you gain more wisdom and insight not just about the world we live in, but about your feelings and experiences as well. As a result, you will now be able to develop more constructive ways of dealing with your personal issues. Eventually, you will be able to achieve a perfect balance of reason and emotion in your life.

Aside from a healthy self-perception and interactions with other people, your personal health can also be improved once you have opened your third eye. Since you are relatively at peace, your stress levels will go down and will remain at a manageable level during distressing situations. As a result, you may even lower the risk of being affected by high blood pressure and depression. Suffering from minor aches such as upset stomachs and migraines will also be lessened considerably. Some people even claim that their skin has become brighter and younger-looking after awakening their third eye.

Dealing with a Blocked Third Eye Chakra

There are times when people experience a blockage in their ajna chakra after they have successfully opened their third eye. This usually stems from doubt that originated either from another person or from within themselves. Major negative experiences in life, such as the death of a loved one, divorce, or sudden illnesses, can also contribute to the blockage. Even transitional periods like birthdays or moving on to a new job can have large impact on the flow of energy to your chakra.

In order for you to conduct a self-assessment of this condition, here are the common signs of a blockage in the ajna chakra:

- Loss of direction and purpose life

- Indecisiveness over big or small matters

- Loss of motivation especially at work

- Paranoia

Physical symptoms may also manifest as a blocked third eye continues to be unresolved. This includes discomfort in the eyes, migraines, pain in sinus cavities, and backaches.

Blockages can happen to enlightened people due to one life-altering event, or an accumulation of small triggering moments that eventually become too much to handle. Experiencing this during your journey of psychic development is only a temporary setback, not a permanent affliction. There are various ways to heal yourself and get back your third back into its optimal condition, such as:

- **Add chakra foods into your diet**

  It's recommended that basic chakra foods are included in your diet regardless of whether or not you are suffering from a third eye blockage. The list includes every fruit and vegetable, wholegrain food products, and healthy fats. Eating these on a regular basis will ensure the steady flow of energy across different chakras.

  There are, however, specific food items that are more effective in alleviating problems associated with the ajna chakra. For example, dark chocolate is particularly effective in increasing concentration as well enhancing clarity in your thoughts and emotions. It is also high in magnesium—an essential element in lowering your stress levels. Furthermore, dark chocolate has been proven through scientific research to be a great mood booster since it signals the brain to release serotonin, which is also known as the happy hormone.

- **Keep purple crystals and precious stones nearby**

Purple is the color associated with the third eye, so keeping accessories made of crystals or gemstones within this color range can promote the healing process. For people who are always on the go, wearing a necklace with a purple crystal pendant or a pair of purple stud earrings is advisable. The closer it is to the ajna chakra, the more effective it will be in preventing or removing the blockage.

- **Meditate while doing yoga poses**

Balancing the energy in your chakras can be done by incorporating certain yoga poses into your meditation routine. The Eagle Pose and the Child Pose are two of the most recommended positions for beginners since they do not require much flexibility or experience.

During the course of the meditation, you must focus again on the location of your third eye. This time, however, try conjuring images of a purple ball of light and energy floating in front of you. Continue breathing in and out until the sphere begins glowing brighter and warmer. This signifies the negative energies and thoughts being purged out of your system. You are ready to end the session when you start feeling lighter and more receptive to the positive energies that are associated with the third eye chakra.

- **Say affirmations to yourself**

Affirmations are words or phrases that people say to eliminate negative thoughts and feelings, and then replace them with more positive and constructive ones. When thinking of affirmations to say to yourself, try to align them with your basic purpose in life and general interests. For example, you may try repeating under your breath this sentence, "I live everyday under the guidance of my third eye." As you continually say this throughout the day, the meaning behind the sentence will become assimilated into your subconscious mind. From there on, you may also consider saying this mantra during your meditation.

Healing the third eye after a blockage is a simple, straightforward process. If you need further encouragement on setting your ajna chakra back into its ideal condition, just remember that achieving enlightenment is the key to a more fulfilling life. As you become more attuned with your spiritual side, the greater opportunities there are to continually improve your psychic abilities.

Chapter 4 – Understanding Clairvoyance and the Various Methods of Developing Your Psychic Sight

Have you experienced having visions of events that you have not witnessed beforehand? Does your mind seem to solve visual puzzles without much effort on your behalf? Have you ever been told that you have an overactive imagination, only for your so-called imaginations to be proven accurate? If you have answered yes to any of these questions, then you might be gifted with clairvoyance or psychic sight.

A clairvoyant "sees" images and symbols in their minds, which can then be interpreted to give them an understanding of real-world events and problems. When read correctly, the clairvoyant can gain deeper insights into important matters that may or may not affect them directly. Oftentimes, sensitive people who have not yet fully realized their gifts may not put much thought into this special ability. They tend to pass this off as a mere by-product of their creative minds.

The way the media depicts clairvoyance also lessens the chances of people discovering this ability on their own. On-screen psychics tend to be exaggerated in their portrayal of how these visions appear to them. Because of this, someone who may be in possession of this ability might choose to downplay their personal experiences, believing that it should be more dramatic and exciting than merely seeing a vague form in their mind's eye.

In real life, however, clairvoyance is a subtle art of seeing and interpreting these visions. It takes years of practice to completely master this skill since the images do not tell the whole story in one go. A series of visual bursts usually are received over a certain period of time before the full story is uncovered. The eyes do not even need to remain closed to tap into this ability. The images typically appear in the blink of an eye, so there are times when an inexperienced clairvoyant may not be able to decode the meaning behind them.

Characteristics of a Clairvoyant Person

If you believe that you might be a clairvoyant, here is a list of the common signs and symptoms that clairvoyants typically experience:

- **You have a deep connection with artwork and other beautiful objects**

  Clairvoyants have a penchant for surrounding themselves with beautiful things. They can be absolutely moved when viewing paintings, sculptures and other works of art. Their appreciation of beauty, however, does not end on the surface level only.

  Clairvoyants find themselves empathizing with the creator of the artwork. In their minds, they can envision the hours of hard work that the painter had put into their masterpiece. They feel connected emotionally with the artists through the feelings that the artist had while in the process of making the masterpiece. As a result, the spirituality of the clairvoyant is further enriched by their empathy with fellow sensitive types of people.

- **You can visualize events and symbols with ease**

Since they are naturally disposed to rely on their sight, a clairvoyant's psychic abilities often manifest in bursts of scenes and imagery in their mind's eye. The meanings behind each vision may be symbolic, prophetic, or even literal, but whichever it is, experiencing this means that the clairvoyant's mind is trying to make sense of the psychic information that is being received.

As an illustration, an average clairvoyant may suddenly see a field of flowers before them, only for it to disappear within the next second. The mind is flooded with varying shapes, colors, and textures, but no apparent meaning is overtly presented right away. It may seem strange at first for the clairvoyant, but with regular meditation and mind training, the images will begin to make more sense until finally, the clairvoyant is able to decipher the message that is being conveyed.

- **You frequently have vivid dreams**

Clairvoyants tend to dream and daydream more often than normal humans. The content of their dreams is typically remembered in greater detail with lots of brilliant colors and sharp images. Plenty of symbols also make an appearance during their dreams and daydreams.

In some cases, a clairvoyant's dream can have a prophetic element to it. The symbols that repeat across several dreams may suddenly make an appearance in the real world. Their presence in the dreams might have been a forewarning about the upcoming events that have significance to the clairvoyant's life.

To better interpret dreams and the symbols that appear in them, training the mind is highly recommended. When fully trained, clairvoyants may be able to quickly interpret and uncover the meanings behind their dreams, and then understand how the messaged within their dreams applies to themselves and the people around them.

- **You experience psychic flashes**

Psychic flashes are sparks or spheres of light that appear suddenly in the clairvoyant's peripheral vision. Sometimes, these lights signify the presence of spirit guides—ephemeral and typically incorporeal entities that guide or protect humans. However, for clairvoyants, psychic flashes happen as well whenever another being from a different dimension is trying to contact them or share information with them. The flow of energy directed to them takes the form of light spheres or sparks since their psychic abilities are more attuned with their vision.

Other than balls of light, psychic flashes may also be seen as shadows that seem to float and disappear in the corner of the eye. These may also be visible in a person's aura.

- **You can sense things from a great distance**

Due to their heightened sense of sight, clairvoyants can identify disturbances in the psychic and physical worlds. These sensations do not have to be visual in nature. It can be feelings of dread during random points of the day, or an unexplainable excitement over something that cannot be put into words.

The media sometimes take their creative licenses to the next level by making on-screen clairvoyants have the ability to see through walls or objects. This is certainly not the case for real-life psychics. Typically, they are able to pick up on visual cues that the normal human senses would not have picked up. The subconscious mind immediately recognizes them, but it may take a while before the conscious mind figures out what the stimuli is.

- **You easily make connections between people, things, or ideas**

Clairvoyants have the natural ability to understand how different matters connect with one another. In terms of problem solving, they have a higher level of spatial awareness so manipulating shapes and puzzles comes easy for them. As a result, they see the bigger picture immediately, letting them solve the problem quicker than other people.

This does not translate to word or audio puzzles, however. If clairvoyants do train hard, they might be able to translate these stimuli into something that can be processed by their mind's eye. This can be achieved through meditation and other techniques that will be discussed later on.

When it comes to a sense of direction, clairvoyants also have an advantage since they can easily make a mental map of a certain location. This is similar to the special perception skill called the eagle's eye, wherein a person can view a scene or location as if they are flying over it. Clairvoyants make use of their mental maps to find connections between places, events, and ideas—an ability that comes in handy when they are trying to search for someone or something that is missing.

Developing Your Clairvoyance

Much like any other skill, practice is key in developing your psychic abilities. When it comes to clairvoyance, there are seven ways to level up your skills:

1. **Use crystals to open the third eye**

    Parapsychologists recommend budding clairvoyants to use quartz and lapis lazuli in aiding the process of opening the third eye. These crystals and precious stones must be laid close by, or even worn during meditation. While asleep, you may also opt to place them over your forehead in order to harness their energies while you are at rest. By having them around you, these objects can serve as a reminder of your objective and realign your focus on developing your skills as a clairvoyant.

2. **Access the third eye chakra through visualization practice**

Once you have opened your third eye, you can practice harnessing the energy from the ajna chakra by doing visualizations. Start by conjuring up images of specific scenes or locations, such as a piano recital or a sunny beach in Hawaii. From there, visualize smaller details like the style of the gown worn by the pianist, or a seashell that has been washed ashore.

The key to this exercise is keeping the eyes closed during the entire session. This will lessen the possibility of being distracted, as well as maintain your focus on the object or scenery in your mind's eye. If you find this activity to be too difficult, try staring first for at least thirty seconds at a picture of the image you are going to visualize. Then, close your eyes and recreate the picture in your mind. Hold it in there for ten seconds before moving on to the smaller details.

3. **Analyze your dreams**

Writing down your dreams in a journal is a great way to assess how well you are doing in terms of remembering details and interpreting the meaning behind them. To start this habit, prepare a pen and a pad of paper, and place them within an arm's reach, preferably on your nightstand beside your bed. As you lay down, ask yourself questions that need intuitive responses. Repeat the questions until you have drifted off to sleep.

When you wake up, grab the pen and pad of paper to document as many details as you can remember about the dream you just had. If you cannot remember anything, or if you did not have any dream at all, write down instead the first few thoughts you have upon waking up.

Continue this practice daily until you begin to notice similarities in your dreams, and the underlying messages that your dreams are trying to convey.

4. Play memory games

This type of activity offers a challenge to your ability to visualize things. You may start by visualizing each card as it gets turned over. Doing so will help open your third eye chakra.

Another way of developing your visualization is by placing ten objects on the table and memorizing what each looks like, how each feels on the palm of your hand, and where exactly they are placed. After some time, turn away from the table, and write down the details that you remember. This is an excellent assessment of how well you can retain information especially the tiny bits that everyone else may ignore.

5. Meditate regularly

Refining your psychic abilities can be achieved through meditation since its primary goal is to clear the mind. If done well, meditation improves the flow of energy to the chakras, thereby opening the third eye. When the powers of the third eye have been activated, you will notice a significant increase in the quality of your visualizations.

6. Conduct a blind reading

Blind reading is done with use of a card system that serves as tool in refocusing a clairvoyant's energy into answering questions that require their psychic abilities. Here is a step-by-step guide that you may follow in order to conduct a blind reading session:

a. Sit down in a chair before laying down three blank cards on top of a desk.

b. Think of one question that needs to be answered.

c. Write down on each card one possible answer to your question.

d. Turn over the cards so that they are facing down on the desk.

e. Shuffle the position of the cards without turning them over.

f. Brush your hands over each card. Try to sense the energy each one is giving off. Assess which of the three you are leaning more towards selecting. Relax, and take your time in making your decision.

g. When you have your chosen your preferred card, flip the cards over again. Read the answer written on the card you have selected. If you are a true clairvoyant, then it is highly likely that is the right answer to your initial question.

7. Increase the frequency of vibration

High vibration is required to receive messages that are spiritual and psychic in nature. You can increase the vibration of energy within you by focusing on activities that make you happy and repel negative energy. As the vibration increases, the channels dedicated to these messages becomes clearer. When the pathway towards your minds remains clear, the amount of detail relayed to you increases as well.

Clairvoyance is a difficult psychic ability to master, but those who are willing to train can benefit from the many enhancements that the skill can bring into the daily and spiritual life of the person. Since the signs and symptoms tend be subtle, many people sadly end up ignoring their gift altogether.

How could you tell if a vision is something out of your imagination only, or if it is an actual psychic message? The main determining factor is the level of control you have over these visions. When you cannot control the image or the content of the message, then what you are seeing is originating from another entity or another dimension. You are not creating these thoughts. You are not responsible for what the message is. You are not trying at all; the visions just appear in your mind's eye.

There is also a wide variability in terms of the manifestations of this psychic ability. No two clairvoyants are alike. The visions received by one clairvoyant may differ greatly from what another clairvoyant receives. Every scene or symbol may have a different meaning for each clairvoyant, depending on the context of the situation and previous life experiences.

Through regular training and meditation, you can unlock the maximum level of your ability as a clairvoyant. As a result, you will begin to gain a deeper understanding of how these visions relate to you, those around you, and even the future.

Chapter 5 – Understanding the Sixth Sense

Most humans utilize their five senses - sight, sound, smell, taste, and touch - to receive information from their surroundings and navigate through their day-to-day lives. For psychics, however, they also have another way of perceiving information - the sixth sense.

The name itself is not entirely accurate, since the sixth sense is not only one ability. Instead, it is a group of intuitive abilities that allow a person to receive information from other planes of existence, and then process said information through their inner minds.

There are four main types of intuitive abilities: clairvoyance, clairaudience, claircognizance, and clairsentience. The most well-known of them is clairvoyance, which is the ability see psychic visions, symbols, and images that may or may not have precognitive elements to them. The other three intuitive senses will be discussed further in this chapter.

Psychic people may possess more than one intuitive ability. In fact, there are some individuals who have reported having all forms of the sixth sense. Even rarer are those people who have honed all these intuitive abilities along with other psychic abilities, such as psychography or telepathy. They have managed to achieve such great feats of psychic development through their devotion and discipline in training their abilities to the full extent.

As such, it is important for you to learn how to develop the different intuitive abilities that you might possess. Knowing the various ways of maximizing your gifts can be beneficial not only for you, but for the people around you as well.

What Is Clairaudience?

A person who can perceive sounds through their psychic consciousness is called a clairaudient. When you develop this ability to its maximum capacity, you can hear other living beings and spiritual entities with a high level of clarity and accuracy.

Manifestations of this ability can happen as early as from the time you are born. As such, there are certain individuals who go through their entire lives without fully realizing that spirits are communicating with them through their clairaudient ability.

Many people report that they first noticed their special abilities through a persistent ringing in their ears. For many, there had also been a shift in pressure within the ear canals, leading them to feel a buzzing inside their heads, or even loud popping noises. When this ability is fully developed, a clairaudient individual will be able to hear actual voices inside their head as the spirits begin to be drawn closer to them.

More often than not, the spirit voices that clairaudients can hear are not saying things that are malicious or disruptive to you other or other living beings. Oftentimes, they can even sound more rational than your own thoughts. They tend to be compassionate about the plights of humans, and their voices are gentle and sincere.

Characteristics of a Clairaudient Person

At first glance, it might seem that being clairaudient is awfully similar to experiencing hallucinations - something that is frequently associated with people suffering from mental illness. Differentiating a true clairaudient from a mentally ill individual becomes easier if you know which points to examine. Even though both conditions can involve a person hearing voices inside their head, the similarities between these two end there. Here is a list of the common signs that indicate if you are clairaudient or not:

- **You have a habit of talking to yourself**

  Clairaudients can usually find comfort in hearing their own voices when they need a boost of courage, when they are trying to absorb information, or when they are caught up in their own thoughts. What separates these personal talks from standard coping mechanisms is the quality of responses that you may get inside your head.

  For example, while trying to solve a problem, you repeat the key information about the situation to yourself. During the course of the problem-solving process, you might be receiving suggestions inside your head. If these responses sound like well thought-out ideas that you would not have considered yourself under normal circumstances, then you might actually be receiving guidance from a spirit. Furthermore, you are not hearing them through your ears, but rather through your psychic consciousness.

- **You frequently hear ringing or buzzing noises**

Oftentimes, it is not actual words that inexperienced clairaudients hear. Since the level of the psychic perception is not high enough for a proper "conversation", the messages of the spirits will not be received in their original form. Instead, the sounds can end up being muddled and might get lost with the other frequencies that the clairaudient is exposed to.

In other cases, buzzing and ringing sounds may also be the spirits' way of getting your attention. If the noise lasts for a brief moment only but repeats over and over again for a specific duration of time, then this might be a signal from the spirits, indicating that you need to pay attention to what they have to say at that moment.

- **You can hear conversations, voices, or even whispering from a distance**

This differs from a heightened sense of hearing in terms of the actual source of the sounds being heard from far away. If those sounds are made by a real living person from a distance, then it may only be a case of sensitive ears.

However, if you cannot pinpoint the probable source within your surroundings, then the sounds are likely coming to your through meta-physical means. Should this be the case, you may ask the spirits to speak in a louder and clearer voice so that you can understand what they are trying to say. Conversely, you may also request them to keep quiet if they are bothering you, since spirits tend to reach out to clairaudients when they are asleep.

- **You hear messages that seem to be directed towards you**

Clairaudient people frequently experience hearing sound bites from the television or radio that seem to be applicable towards their current situation. It might just be a coincidence if this happens only once, but repeated messages through different means are definitive signs that those instances have been arranged by the spirit who is hoping to relay a message through other people.

- **You are known to give sound advice to people in need**

If people remark how good you are at giving advice, only for you to be surprised since you are not sure how you even arrived at those opinions, then there is a high chance that the spirits are using you to help other people. When you have a high level of spirituality, you may become more receptive about the idea of allowing other entities to borrow your abilities for time to time since they do not have the capabilities to do it on their own. As such, they use you as their "mouthpiece" to this world, or in some cases, they may also guide you in writing down their messages through another psychic ability called psychography.

- **You willingly comfort others**

  When benevolent spirits choose you as their vessels in communicating with the physical world, you will develop urges to help out others and comfort them in times of need. This may also occur without your knowledge, but more often than not, it is merely a case of being influenced by the types of spirits that tap into your clairaudience.

- **You suddenly get inspired by doing typically mundane tasks**

  Clairaudient people report experiencing breakthroughs while doing simple day-to-day tasks, such as eating, showering, or driving. During the time they are doing those activities, their minds are not trying to come up with possible ideas or solutions. However, out of the blue, a likely answer appears inside their head as if it had been there all along.

  These insights are not products of your unconscious mind. Instead, the spirits had taken advantage of your lack of awareness during those times, and slipped through unnoticed to tell you of their suggestions, or to guide you to arriving at the right answers.

Developing Your Clairaudience

Clairaudient psychics can develop their skills in order to gain control over the sounds they hear. Since the spirits tend to be inconsistent in terms of their delivery, clairaudients must further enhance their psychic abilities so that brief and sometimes vague messages from the spirit can be converted into understandable and useful information.

There are several simple exercises that you can do to increase the sensitivity of your psychic hearing. When you practice your abilities, think of yourself as an antenna that can pick up signals of psychic nature just by using your special intuitive abilities.

You should also remember that hearing something through psychic means is vastly different from hearing sounds through your physical ears. For the former, the voices, noises, or even musical sounds are more subtle than their counterparts here in the living world. This is why exercising your clairaudience is vital to your development as a psychic.

The main goal of these exercises is to push your psychic hearing ability to its limits, and go beyond those limits, if possible. Though these exercises are simple and easy to do, you must remember to practice regularly since the results or changes in your abilities will not be readily evident during your first few attempts. Be patient with yourself, and soon you will notice the gradual improvements in your psychic abilities.

1. **Listen**

   It may sound counterintuitive, since you hear psychic sounds through your mind, but the simplest way of increasing your sensitivity is by training your physical ears. Close your eyes and listen closely to the various sounds in your environment. Try to discern the tiny sounds and noises that you typically do not pay attention to. This may be the sound of rustling leaves as the wind blows through them. Or it may even be the noises of passing cars out in the street. When you hear these sounds, identify their source and differentiate each one from the symphony of sounds during a normal day.

As you become more acquainted with listening to the physical sounds around you, you can take this a step further by trying to guess what is causing the subtle sounds you are hearing. A light ringing, or a soft humming, what may be causing these sounds? You don't have to go and find out if you are correct. The point of this exercise is simply to improve your ear's sensitivity, not to increase the accuracy of your intuition.

2. Listen to music

Any type of music may be used during practice, but the best option for clairaudients is classical music. Pieces classified as such are typically just instrumental, so the chances of being distracted by the voice of the singer or the message of the song's lyrics will be eliminated.

Before starting this exercise, look for a place where you can sit down comfortably while playing music. Make sure that there will no likelihood of you being interrupted during the course of this activity.

Once you are set, play the music and listen carefully to its melody. After a minute or two, choose one instrument to focus on. Typical instruments used in classical music are the violin and the piano. For example, you can identify the notes being played by the violin. Listen to the flow of music coming from the violin while trying to downplay the rest of the instruments.

If you cannot seem to focus on one instrument, slowly breathe in and out. This will realign your concentration so you can have another go. Once you have managed to follow the violin for at least a minute, switch to another instrument and do the same for the next minute. Repeat these steps until the music ends.

When you do this exercise, you are actually working on two things. First, you are increasing the level of your sensitivity towards different sounds that are playing at the same time. When you are hearing psychic information, the sounds from the physical world will not be silenced. Instead, you will hear these gentle voices from spirits alongside the normal level of noises during your typical day.

Second, this exercise pushes the limits of how much you can concentrate on one thing only, when there are so many other things going on the same time. This will test if you can focus on what really matters rather than the extraneous sounds that might distract you from receiving spiritual messages.

3. Imagine different sounds

A great way of exercising your intuitive abilities is by practicing your imagination. By doing so, you are expanding your mind and improving your receptivity towards the different types of sounds that you might hear from another dimension.

The important prerequisite for this exercise is a quiet room where you can sit down and focus on your imagination. When you have found such a place and managed to find the most comfortable spot for you, begin the exercise by coming up with different sounds inside your head. It can be something musical, such as guitar strings being plucked one by one. You may also choose to play your favorite song inside your head. Distinct sounds that you normally hear, such as the humming of your refrigerator or the different noises that construction tools make are excellent sounds to imagine as well.

For more advanced practitioners, imagining the sounds of voices is a more challenging task since we cannot simply make up these sounds without patterning it after someone we know. Try imagining simple human sounds, such as laughter, or a quick greeting, before moving on to more complex sounds.

4. Meditate

Meditation is key for developing various psychic abilities. This applies to clairaudience as well since you are tapping into your inner mind whenever you use this ability.

The objective of meditation is to clear your mind and bring your mind and body down into a relaxed state. To do this, find a place where you can be alone with your thoughts. Sit down or lie down on the floor while evening out your breathing. If you have any favorite meditation techniques that can get you to the right state of mind, then apply them as well. Try to incorporate this task into your daily routine. At least 15 minutes per day is recommended in order to make daily meditation in to a habit.

When you feel you are ready for the next step, you have to extend the duration of your meditation sessions. During the course of this activity, try asking questions that you might have for your spirit guides or even your higher self. Indicate as well that you prefer to receive their responses through your psychic hearing, since the spirits have various ways of answering your questions while you are meditating. If they respond, it will usually be in the form of words, vague sounds, or even music.

Clairaudience is a wonderful ability to possess. It may be scary at first, but once you begin recognizing the new sounds you are hearing, then you will gradually embrace the gifts that have been awakened within you.

Claircognizance

Have you ever felt that something is about to happen out of the blue, and later on found out that you were right? For some people, this may only be a case of you following your gut feeling. However, our instincts can be wrong, and therein lies the main difference between the gut feeling and claircognizance.

A claircognizant individual is capable of knowing information without being able to explain how he is able to know in the first place. Furthermore, their knowledge about a situation, or the intentions behind an action, or even future events are consistently, sometimes scarily, accurate.

Characteristics of a Claircognizant Person

There are various ways to tell if you are gifted with claircognizance. By knowing which signs to look for, you can determine if the knowledge you possess is not only coming from your own mind, but rather from other entities who are trying to guide you throughout your life.

- **Your gut instincts are always correct**

  All human beings possess instincts from the moment we are born. There are also instincts that we learn as we go through life, such as those we learn from how we are raised, to those we learn by making mistakes. Since these gut instincts are primarily rooted upon our past experiences, there is no guarantee that they will always be right.

  For example, your instincts may be telling you not to interact with dogs since you were bitten once when you were a child. That message is valuable for your survival and can be logical at times, especially when you encounter a particularly aggressive breed. However, it can be inaccurate at times as well because not all dogs are predisposed to biting strangers.

In contrast, claircognizant people have instincts that speak only of the truth. For example, despite not meeting yet or not hearing much about the new guy that your friend is dating, your claircognizant abilities might be telling you that something is terribly off with that person. You have no way of knowing for sure if you are correct or not at the time. However, later on, you might learn from your friend that they have stopped dating that guy because he was an abusive person.

- **You can easily tell if someone is lying**

Claircognizant people are able to detect when someone is telling a lie, even simple and little white lies. In some cases, recognizing insincerity in the expressed emotions or sentiments is also within the scope of the abilities of claircognizants.

This ability goes beyond the normal human skill of reading other people's body language. Liars can be very good at hiding the tells and quirks of their face, voice, or bodily gestures, but such mastery over their words and actions cannot hide away their attempts of deception from the psychic sense of knowing.

- **You think of random ideas or solutions without prompt**

When you frequently come up with thoughts or ideas out of the blue, then these may have originated from signals that your inner mind has processed and recognized to be true. For example, these can be simple thoughts such as going back to check if you have properly locked the door or not. If you are claircognizant, then you will find out that you have indeed left the door unlocked.

Again, this ability may be similar to gut instincts. However, if you have repeatedly avoided repercussions or bad consequences by following these random thoughts or ideas, then there is a high chance that this is brought about by your special abilities instead.

It should be noted that these messages will not come to you at all times. The randomness means that you might receive a message any time of the day. The message will not always be explicitly clear either, but if you pay attention to these msessages, then you might be able to glean off the intent behind the message. Oftentimes, these are warnings or pieces of advice that could prevent bad things from happening to you or those around you.

Sometimes, this ability works best while you are asleep. There are claircognizants who have experienced waking up with the solutions to their problems right in their head. This indicates that your inner mind is hard at work even if you are not conscious at the time.

- **You can predict events**

  Beyond what is known and what is currently happening, claircognizant individuals are capable of predicting the occurrence and even the outcome of events. Furthermore, they achieve such feats without any form of basis for their inferences about the outcome, or evidence of prior knowledge about the said events.

  Under normal circumstances, drawing conclusions and making decisions is based on facts and hard evidence available for the person to measure and analyze. However, with claircognizance, the person can skip this long process, and arrive at accurate deductions and predictions without much mental effort. They simply just know what is going to happen in the end.

  There are various basic examples of this ability at work. You may be able to predict the outcome of an application that you or a friend has taken. Or you may be able to know beforehand that a major life event is going to happen to someone else, thereby giving you the chance to forewarn them of what is about to come.

Developing Your Claircognizance

Before delving into the different ways of developing your claircognizant skills, you must remember that when it comes to this psychic ability, you should let go of whatever notions you have about reason and logic. Those two concepts do not apply to what claircognizance can allow people to do. If you clear your mind and open yourself up to new possibilities, then you can soon reap the benefits of a well-developed ability of psychic knowing.

1. Recognize and appreciate the manifestations of your ability

This may sound like something you should be naturally doing at this point, but not everyone who is blessed with claircognizance takes the time to embrace their special ability. At the most basic level, you should remember that you can only fully develop claircognizance if you believe that you do have this ability. Some psychic abilities are easier to prove and are more obvious to a casual observer than even to yourself.

Living your life as a claircognizant person requires for you to set aside your rationality and understand that your inner mind can and will give you the right answers when you need it to. This does not mean that you should totally abandon logical thinking or completely ignore hard evidence. It just means that you have to trust yourself and the knowledge that you have, even if there is apparent proof to support it.

Developing claircognizant skills does not only stop at recognition. You also have to act on the intuitive messages that you are receiving. Take responsibility for them and execute on the advice you receive whenever applicable.

At the start, you may have a million and questions as to why you should be acting on these seemingly random thoughts. However, as you continue to develop your psychic abilities, you will learn how valuable your intuition can be in the success of your personal interactions and day-to-day living.

2. Request assistance from your spirit guides

Spirit guides exist to guide us throughout our lives. As such, they can be invaluable companions in attaining success on your quest towards psychic development.

You can get in touch with them through meditation. Invite them for a simple conversation and request their guidance as you continue to exercise your various psychic abilities.

If you have not done this before, here is a step-by-step guide on how to communicate with your spirit guides:

a. Meditate. Look for a place where you can relax and free you mind from your worries and distractions. Focus also on your breathing. Make sure that your breaths are measured and deep.

b. Think about your intentions. In this case, you intend to develop your claircognizant ability into its full capacity.

c. Invite your spirit guides to join you. You may say this out loud, or you may express this inside your head only. When you do this, try to imagine your spirit guide sitting down directly across you. Do not concentrate on how they actually appear. Think of them as a simple form of energy that has made their presence known to you.

d. Communicate your thoughts and feelings. If you do not know where to start, you can begin by telling them how excited you are about embarking on this journey with them. From there, share with your spirit guides your expectations from them about helping you to develop your ability.

e. When you have spoken your mind, express your gratitude to your spirit guides. You may also commit to them that their guidance will always be welcome and appreciated.

If you want to ensure the success of your communion with your spirt guide, then you can try diffusing essential oils while you are meditating. This can increase your concentration, and further relax your body and mind.

3. Try your hand at psychography

Psychography, also known as automatic writing, is a separate psychic ability from claircognizance, but it may be used in the development of the latter. This is achieved by incorporating automatic writing whenever you communicate with your spirit guides.

Psychography is the ability to channel other spiritual entities and receive messages from them. The information gained from the non-physical dimensions is then translated into writing. During the course of this action, the person himself has no control whatsoever over what is going to be written. They are merely being used by the spirits to relay their messages.

Practicing psychography as a way to develop claircognizance will let you record your interactions with your spirit guides, and therefore be able to assess later on the authenticity of the messages you are receiving through your inner mind.

You may begin this exercise by grabbing a pen and a piece of paper. You may also want to ensure that the place where you will be doing this is quiet and away from potential interruptions.

When you are ready, ask your spirit guides or even your higher self a question. Wait for a while as you feel the energy in your body coursing through you. Then, when you feel the impulse to write down something, follow that instinct. The words don't need to have any meaning at this point. Even gibberish language is acceptable. Just let your pen write down whichever thought or idea you are receiving.

Many claircognizants do not see the point of doing this exercise at first, since they do not believe that they are equipped to do psychography. However, the times when you not getting any meaningful answers can still be helpful in developing your claircognizant abilities. Your subconscious is being cleared out, and this in turn will make you more receptive to messages from the spiritual world.

Over time and with continued practice, you will start receiving information that will make sense or be applicable to the question you have asked earlier. This means that you have managed to strengthen your claircognizant skills, and soon you will begin receiving clearer messages through your intuition.

4. Practice visualization exercises

Using visualization for the development of claircognizant abilities is not merely done through meditation. You have to incorporate journaling as well since this will help you to create a better view of your current life, and what your life will be like when you have mastered claircognizance.

To start this exercise, get yourself a pen and a journal. You may also use a pad of paper, but for better safekeeping, a bound journal is the recommended option.

Describe in written words how your life would change once you have fully developed your claircognizance. This will serve as your primary objective for these exercises.

Next, write down about an actual day in your life wherein you had a sudden idea to do something, and by following through with this idea, you gained something positive. For example, one day, you may have had an urge to go and buy a cup of coffee at this local café that you do not usually frequent. While you were lined up in the counter, you ran into your old friend from college, who then gave you a tip about an opening at the company he is working for. That position happens to be your dream job.

For the next part, you have to visualize how claircognizance can further influence your day-to-day life in positive ways. When you meditate, you should focus on the details of how your life could be improved through claircognizance. Absorb these details and let the positive energy flow through you. Imagine exactly how your mind and body would feel when you exhibit signs of your claircognizant abilities.

Repeat these steps every day. Gradually, you will notice an increase in the frequency of claircognizant moments during your day-to-day life.

5. Practice using Zener cards

Zener cards are typically used to develop extrasensory perception or ESP abilities. However, this tool is also applicable for those who want to improve their claircognizance.

You can get Zener cards in physical stores or through online shops. You may also make your own, if you wish to do so. All you need are five index cards and pens of various colors. Draw the following shapes on each card using different colors for each shape: a five-point star, a circle inside a star, a square, a plus sign, and three parallel wavy lines.

When your Zener cards are ready, place them in one pile facing down on the table. Pick one card from the set and place it in front of you while keeping it facing downward.

Imagine the shape depicted on the card. Do not turn it over until you have pictured the shape in your mind. When you are done, flip over the card and check how accurate you are. Take note of the shape in general, and the color of the pen used to draw the shape on the card.

If you do not get it right the first time, do not be disheartened. The main point of this exercise is for you to get over your reliance on your logical thoughts. You do have to overthink it when you are using your claircognizant abilities.

If you want to increase the level of your confidence during your first few tries, you may use two cards only instead of the usual five. This will increase your chances of being accurate to fifty percent. As you go on with this exercise, you can add more Zener cards until you observe an increase in the accuracy of your predictions.

6. Listen to music

Doing this exercise is so simple that you can do it wherever you are playing music or whenever you hear a song playing. For example, while you are driving to work, you can switch on your music player or radio, and try to guess which song will come up next.

If you did not manage to get a correct answer, that is all right since accuracy is not the point of this particular exercise. Instead, the aim of doing this is to open up your intuitive side through music.

In general, music can increase the vibration felt by humans, and the higher the rate of vibration is, the stronger your psychic abilities become. In addition, music inspires creativity in the right side of the brain, which also happens to be where the center of intuition is located.

7. Listen to your intuition when you need to make decisions

The next time you are going to make a decision with a relatively small impact on your life, imagine yourself asking your inner mind for the right answer. Even when you are not sure if that is the correct answer, imagine that your inner knowing already has the answers you are seeking, and trust that the advice has been made with your best interest in mind.

Once you have recognized your intuition as something that can be depended upon, you will be able to tap into your psychic abilities whenever you are facing bigger and tougher issues in your life. The momentum you have built up through your learned habit of depending on your intuition can be key to unlocking the greater potential of your claircognizant abilities.

Having knowledge about matters that you should not have known about in the first place, or events that have not yet happened, cannot be made possible with just the use of your five physical senses. Claircognizance makes it possible for psychics to skip over the tedious process of observing others and the surroundings for clues that still do not guarantee one-hundred-percent accuracy on the resulting conclusions and decisions.

Clairsentience

Clairsentience bears a striking similarity with claircognizance in the sense that they resemble the natural gut instinct of humans. When it comes to claircognizance, the person possesses knowledge about certain matters that they should not have known, or that they have no prior information about. On the other hand, clairsentience allows a person to feel the energy of another person, object, or place in the form of gut feelings. For example, when you pass by a man along the street, you may suddenly feel like you should not trust him. You do not have any knowledge about what kind of person he is, or what he has done before. However, your psychic feeling ability is telling you to stay from that man.

Characteristics of a Clairsentient Person

Clairsentient individuals are able to determine the activation of their special skills by taking note of key changes in the way they live out their day-to-day lives. Since the mere possession of this ability can have a tremendous impact on a person, it is important to learn immediately the ins and outs of clairsentience in order to prevent certain inconveniences in your life. For example, a clairsentient person may feel drained physically and emotionally after going to the mall. Due to the heavy traffic of people there, an inexperienced clairsentient may be absorbing all of those energies—both positive and negative—rendering them exhausted and in need of serious relaxation and meditation.

For you to avoid such instances, and for you to start developing this skill, here is a list of the common signs that indicate whether or not you are clairsentient:

- **You feel inexplicably tired after being with a large group**

  Clairsentients normally feel energy at an intense level. That is why interacting with a large group of people all at once can be an extremely draining activity for them.

  Different people possess various types of energy and emotions, and all of these can bombard the psychic senses of a clairsentient individual. To recover from such an intense sensation, a clairsentient will have to stay away for a while, and recharge through meditation or other forms of relaxation.

- **Your instincts about a person, a place, or a situation are usually accurate**

  If you can accurately sense someone's intention without any explanation for it, then you are likely to be clairsentient. Individuals who show this ability tend to be asked by their friends for advice on their romantic partners.

On a personal level, clairsentient people use this ability to determine who they can trust and who they need to stay away from. Whichever your situation is, having the capacity to do any of this is indicative of your activated psychic ability.

- **You can feel the energy going around a room**

Energy within a room can either be emitted by the people already inside the room or left by the people who were just in the room. This particular fact is the reason why crowded areas can be draining for a clairsentient. To combat the negative effects of such situations, some carry around a protective crystal with them whenever go out in the public. An effective, but relatively cheap option for this is a piece of black tourmaline crystal.

- **You can sense if someone is in a bad mood even when they try to hide it**

General moods and emotions currently felt by a person are within the scope of detection for clairsentient individuals. Without having to rely on body language or other situational cues, people who have this ability can automatically tell if someone is experiencing a bad day. Even if they are hiding behind a big, toothy smile, clairsentients can still manage to see what the person is truly feeling at that moment.

- **You find it difficult to watch or read the news**

  Clairsentients are known to be averse to news show and the newspaper. Since they can pick up energies from both living beings and non-living objects, listening or reading about distressful events can be particularly draining for clairsentients. Just by merely reading a story about a flash flood can bring about a deluge of negative energies, which can be terrible for the physical strength and emotional stability of a clairsentient person.

- **You tear up whenever you watch emotional films**

  Similarly, watching films that portray highly emotional characters or depict emotional scenes can be quite exhausting for a clairsentient. These individuals can easily sense the pain felt by the characters, even if such intense feelings are only fabricated by the actors for that particular scene.

- **You feel random emotions out of the blue**

  If have experienced a sudden rush of emotions without any sort of explanation for it, then you might be a clairsentient. Others may tell you that this is only a result of changes in hormones, or they may suggest that you are faking it. However, clairsentience can manifest in this manner as well. There are a lot of energies and spirits in our environment. This leaves the clairsentient particularly vulnerable to emotional changes.

- **You are highly sensitive towards your surroundings**

Do you ever notice that sudden changes in your environment disrupt your disposition and ruin your mood for the day? Does clutter bother you more than the average person? If you answered yes to these questions, then you might have activated the ability of psychic feeling. Clairsentience connects people to their surroundings on a much deeper level because of the new energies that are now flowing into the chakras. For example, the energy and vibrations of a house can influence the final decision of a clairsentient person who wishes to buy it.

- **You can easily empathize with other's pain**

Having the ability to pick up on other people's pain is common trait possessed by all clairsentients. It is not limited only to emotional pain, which empaths can also sense. Physical pain can also be intensely felt by clairsentients. For example, imagine that while walking out on the street, you come across a homeless man sitting on the curbside. When you gaze upon him, you do not only feel sadness or loneliness, but also a throbbing pain in your stomach, indicating the man is experiencing hunger pangs. Due to this capacity, many clairsentients avoid going to hospitals since it can be a quite distressful activity for them.

- **You are often told that you are quite sensitive**

  Have you been described by other people as overly sensitive, or maybe even as empathic? If you are clairsentient, then they are correct since people who possess this psychic ability are natural empaths. You can feel things that are beyond what normal humans can sense.

Developing Your Clairsentience

If you believe that you possess the ability to perceive information through the feelings evoked by other people, objects, and certain places, then you may consider going through the following methods of further developing and strengthening your psychic abilities.

1. **Clear out your surroundings**

   By nature, clairsentient individuals can be easily influenced by the state of their environment. Moving a table decoration by even a single inch can have an impact on their perception, and might mess up how well they receive information from their surroundings.

   Therefore, before further pursuing your target of developing your clairsentience, it is important to clear out the clutter and other unnecessary objects within the surrounding areas of thc place where you intend to exercise your psychic ability.

You can begin this by first identifying a space that can be dedicated to you and you alone. In a typical scenario, this could be your own bedroom. However, if you live with someone else, and you do not have separate bed, then it could be just a small corner in your house that you could fill with anything that makes you feel happy and comfortable. This could be simple items such as floor cushions, various crystals and precious stones, and a nice, cozy blanket.

Clairsentient individuals also find objects that are colored green to be helpful in developing their psychic abilities. These can make them feel more connected with nature, and thus further ground them with the current environment.

Burning sage and diffusing its scent around the room can also clear out the negative energies lurking in that place. After you have done this, you can set the new atmosphere for your spot so that it will be filled with light and positive energy.

Setting up your own space is valuable for improving your clairsentience. It will also allow you meditate and conduct psychic exercises without having to go through the trouble of seeking a new place every time you need to practice.

2. Assess your friend's friend or relative

This exercise is done by borrowing a photograph from your friend depicting a family member of theirs, or a friend from another social group. That person should not be someone you have met before, or have heard about frequently.

Look into the picture and concentrate on the person's eyes. Try to sense how they must have been feeling when they were photographed. Sure, their facial expressions can be a dead giveaway, but these can be faked, or they could have been feeling a combination of emotions when the picture was taken. Assess also if you would trust this person if you knew them personally. Do they give off a bad vibe, or do they seem like you two would hit it off?

 After you are done with your evaluation, ask your friend about the accuracy of your assessment. See how closely your findings match up with the actual scenario that was captured by the camera. Find out how well you were able to determine the person's trustworthiness.

Conduct this exercise over and over again, as many times as possible. Eventually, you will get better at reading other people by sensing their feelings and the vibrations they are emitting.

3. Sense the energy being emitted by a personal object

When we value a particular object, or have used it frequently in the past, our energy can be transferred into the object, which will then be absorbed as its own. For example, the more you wear your favorite sweater, the more likely it will have the same type of energy as you have as its owner.

Practicing psychometry—or the ability to read the energy of objects—can be an excellent form of exercise for those who wants to develop the clairsentience ability. Again, you can ask for the help of a friend for this.

Borrow a piece of jewelry or family heirloom from a friend, but make sure that it belongs to someone you do not personally know. It's recommended to use objects that are made of precious metals since they can retain the energy of their owners for a significantly long period of time.

Take a deep breath while rubbing your hands together. When you feel ready, hold the object between your hands for a few minutes. Try to feel if the object is giving off any type of energy. When you do sense something, evaluate if the energy is positive or negative.

After a while, switch your focus to the owner of the object. See if you can sense the energy of that person from the object itself. Evaluate the energy again, but this time, try to sense if the person is naturally happy or humorous, or if they are suffering from bouts of depression. Does the person tend to be calm even in stressful situations, or is the person a tad neurotic?

Once you are done, refer back to your friend to check the accuracy of your observations. Do not be discouraged if you do get things right the first time. If you perform this exercise regularly, soon you would be able to notice a significant increase in the accuracy of your clairsentience.

4. Meditate

Receiving psychic information can be improved further by getting in touch with entities from the spiritual world. The most recommended way of doing this is through meditation.

Meditation is a simple activity that you can and must do every day. All you need is a quiet spot where you can focus your mind and energy into achieving your psychic development objectives. If you have created a personal place beforehand, then the optimal place to meditate would be there.

When you meditate, try imagining yourself in the act of receiving intuitive messages from various spirits, including those assigned to be your personal guides. Picture your mind expanding as you continue to receive these messages effortlessly. After a few minutes, try imagining yourself walking down the street. As you pass by strangers, you are able to sense their feelings and determine if you can trust them or not. That right there is an image of a clairsentient psychic who has completely mastered their abilities.

Meditation also allows you to communicate with your higher self. That entity knows you inside and out, and can therefore contribute vital information as to how you can further improve yourself and your psychic abilities.

5. Create a crystal grid

Crystals are a great way to activate psychic powers and continually provide the right type of energy needed for their further development. For clairsentience, amethyst and fluorite are highly suggested since they are naturally linked with the chakras related to your clairsentient abilities.

To harness the full powers of the crystals, creating a grid out of them is the most effective way. This may sound like a complicated task, but it is so simple that you can actually create your own in just a matter of a few minutes. Here is a quick guideline if you decide to make this your next home project:

a. Buy at least 8 crystals. You can actually buy as many as you want, but for starters 8 to 12 crystals will be sufficient to make a significant impact on your psychic development. You are also free to choose the combinations of crystals for your grid. It can be all fluoride crystals, all amethysts, or a mix of these two crystals. There is essentially no right or wrong combination, so do not be afraid to experiment.

b. Choose one crystal, and place it on the center of the grid. Using this as a focal point, arrange the rest of the crystals in a circular formation around the first piece.

c. As you position each crystal, think of the intention behind this crystal grid. For this purpose, you can say that you intend to receive psychic information through your ability to sense feelings. You can also specify that you want to be more sensitive, and that you want to produce more accurate results.

d. When you are done, you can place the crystal grid you have made in your personal meditation spot, under the bed that you sleep on, or on a table that you regularly pass by.

To increase the effectiveness of the crystals, you may also want to rub essential oils on them before placing them on a grid. Lavender or rose oils are great picks for clairsentience.

In order for the grid to be portable, some people lay down the crystals on a board or a piece of paper. If this will be applicable to your needs, then feel free to do so. What matters most is the circular formation of the crystals, as well as the location where you intend to put the grid.

Anybody can awaken their ability to sense feelings from other people, objects, or places. We are all psychics after all, so in the end, it is only a matter of interest and devotion to the spiritual arts that will spell the difference between self-proclaimed psychics and an average person.

For clairsentience, you can start your psychic development by focusing on carving out a space just for you, and then doing the exercises designed for this particular ability. You can also visit garage sales and antique shops since they are an excellent source of objects that you can practice on.

Lesser Known Intuitive Abilities

Aside from the four primary types of intuitive senses, there also exists two lesser known forms of the sixth sense that do not get much attention from budding psychics. Clairgustance and clairsalience are the psychic equivalents of our sense of taste, and smell, respectively. They may not be as flashy as clairvoyance or claircognizance, but when utilized properly, these abilities can be of great help to the day-to-day life of the psychic.

Clairgustance and clairsalience typically are awakened in conjunction with each other, reflecting how our physical senses relate to one another as well. There is also a high chance that you already possess these abilities if you have keen senses of taste and smell. This, however, does not mean that all psychics will automatically have both of these skills when one of these abilities is activated. They can remain mutually exclusive skills, though the chances of this happening are quite low.

People with the ability of clairgustance, or psychic taste, receive information from the spirit world through their mouth. This is exemplified by mediums who suddenly get a taste of cigarettes in their mouths when trying to connect with a departed soul who used to smoke back when they were alive. For those practicing the healing arts, clairgustance can be helpful in making a diagnosis and suggesting treatments for their patients.

Clairsalient psychics, on the other hand, perceive information in the form of distinct smells coming from no apparent cause within their environments. This particular ability is actually pretty common among those who are in touch with their intuition, but it tends to be overlooked due to its subtle nature. When you suddenly smell your grandfather's cologne during his burial, this is clairsalience at work. Your loved one is trying to make their presence known from the spirit world, and sometimes the only way they can do so is by signaling you through the smells that you have associated with them.

There are several ways to develop your clairgustance and clairsalience abilities. This can be achieved through exercises or through the help of your spirit guides. Many experts, however, recommend balancing first the energy flow in and out of your throat chakra. According to parapsychologists who have studied how each chakra relates to psychic abilities, clairgustance and clairsalience, along with clairaudience are all linked to the throat chakra, so maintaining a healthy and balanced throat chakra can facilitate the development of these psychic abilities.

You may be having problems with your throat chakra if you are exhibiting the following signs and symptoms:

- Physical conditions in the throat region, such as thyroid problems

- Frequently over-eating and bingeing

- Having trouble explaining what you really mean

- Feeling depressed due to an inability to accurately express yourself

To alleviate such problems, you may clear your throat chakra and get it back to its optimal state through the following methods:

- Eating blueberries since the color blue is associated with this chakra

- Wearing clothes of varying shades of blue

- Writing down your thoughts instead of saying them out loud

- Singing or humming a melody

Aside from maintaining the health of your throat chakra, here is a list of the common and simple ways to develop your clairgustance and clairsalience:

1. Play a guessing game with a friend

Ask a friend to help you train and strengthen your psychic abilities. You can ask them to pick certain food items without letting you know of their choices. Then, while blindfolded, try to assess which food is being presented to you by tasting or smelling the mystery food.

The objective of this exercise is not to guess which food it is without using your senses at all. Instead, this activity serves as a way to fine-tune your sense of taste and smell. After all, the more sensitive your mouth and nose are, the stronger their psychic equivalents become too.

2. Test your abilities in a real-world setting

Another type of training that you can do with a friend is by asking them to eat or drink something while on a phone call with them. There are two ways go about this exercise. You may opt to guess the item they are eating or drinking. Or you may ask your friend to tell you what they have chosen to eat or drink, and then check if you can tune in to their senses.

If you are successful, you will be able to taste or smell the same object as your friend. Do keep in mind that it may take some time before your clairgustance or clairsalience kicks in, especially if you are new at this. Do not also expect a strong flavor or scent since it takes a lot of practice to get yourself to that level of sensitivity.

3. Imagine how food tastes or smells

After you are done honing your senses, you can also develop your clairgustance and clairsalience by imagining what certain foods would taste or smell like, without actually exposing yourself towards that food itself. For example, imagine that you are eating a piece of chocolate. Just the thought of chocolate might be able get your mouth watering since you can remember how pleasant its taste and smell are.

You don't have to limit yourself to food items only. You can also try imagining various distinct flavors and smells, such as alcoholic beverages, toothpaste, or even cigarettes. It would be more effective, however, if you had actually tasted or smelled that object beforehand so that you can have a point of reference for your imagination.

4. Request assistance from spirits

Asking for the help of your spirit guides can be done through meditation or mediumship. For meditation, you have to get your mind and body into a relaxed state before inviting in your spirit guide. From there, you can seek their help in developing your psychic abilities.

Mediumship, on the other hand, involves getting the help of departed family members, or even friends. Find a quiet place where you can commune with the entities of the spiritual world. When you have successfully made contact, ask them to send you a particular scent that can be associated with them, or a taste of the food they used to cook when they were still alive. You may also ask them to send a taste or smell that would remind you of key moments in your life, such as your childhood.

Wait for a few minutes and see if they will grant your request. If they did, you will receive the requested stimuli, which you can then try to identify. Keep in mind, however, that these tend to be subtle, so if you are not careful enough, you might miss out the sensations they are sending to you.

The next time that you taste or smell something out of the blue, take a moment to pause, and assess if such stimuli are being detected by your physical senses, or if they are being perceived through your special intuitive abilities. You may be pleasantly surprised at how quickly you can develop these psychic abilities once you have taken an interest in them.

Chapter 6 – How to View and Understand Auras

Even a long time ago, artists illustrated auras as glowing lights or halos that appeared to surround normal humans or divine beings, such as angels and saints. Though these are masterful products of their creative minds, they are not reflective of how actual auras appear in real life. What these paintings tell us, however, is that among people and beings with a high level of spirituality, their aura seems to be more easily seen or felt by those around them.

Ancient civilizations also have their own distinct ways of recognizing the presence of auras exhibited by their spiritual leaders. Archaeologists have discovered that the early Egyptians illustrated auras in the hieroglyphic markings left in the tombs of their high priests.

Nowadays, scientific methods and tools like Kirlian photography and other electronic equipment with a similar purpose has given us a more accurate picture of what auras actually look like. From these images, we have ascertained that auras are bands of energy that surround a person, and they change in color depending on the mood, personality, health, and spirituality of said person. As such, auras can be quite revealing, especially when read the right way.

Your aura is composed of multiple layers of energy. Each layer changes color at different rates. The outer layer gets altered most frequently since this layer is associated with your current mood, or what you are going through at a specific moment. The inner layer, on the other hand, rarely changes. The colors they show are called the life colors since they remain constant throughout your life.

Meanings of Life Colors

The inner layer of your aura can reveal your purpose in life, the right type of partner for you, the appropriate career path given your strengths and weaknesses, and even your vulnerabilities in terms of health and money. For your guidance, here is a list of the most common life colors, and what each of them reveals:

- **Red**

  People with red auras are more attuned with the physical aspects of life compared to their mental pursuits and spiritual lives. They frequently engage in activities that require the strength and endurance of their bodies, as well as their sensuality. They tend to be more on the extraverted side of the personality spectrum since they live for excitement and adventure.

  Reds prefer to keep in touch with the physical realities of their environment. Being able to use their physical senses—sight, hearing, taste, and touch—makes them feel comfortable within their own worlds.

- **Yellow**

  A yellow aura signifies a carefree, energetic, and almost childlike personality. They seek out fun, but they do not appreciate being the center of attention—preferring to shy away to the sides and lets other people shine.

Individuals with a yellow aura do, however, enjoy bringing happiness to others, as well taking care of their own environment. As such, they thrive well in organizations that promote the conservation of the planet and wildlife.

- **Orange**

Those who have an orange aura live for the thrill of challenges and adventures. They are daredevils by nature since they find excitement when faced with dangerous circumstances. They also actively seek out ways to push themselves to the limit. When asked why they do so, oranges will typically explain that they like risking their lives as a reminder to themselves of the wonders and joys of being alive.

- **Blue**

Blue auras are typically found among the nurturing types of personalities. They are the most supportive people you will ever meet since they not only care about the success of others, but also their emotional and spiritual well-being. Their life purpose lies along the lines of giving without expecting anything in return, and teaching others how to love. Careers that best suit the blues include being a nurse, counselor, or a teacher.

- **Green**

  People exhibiting a green aura are considered to be the most authoritative and smart individuals among a group. They are known for their intellectual prowess since they are capable of processing information quickly and arriving at conclusions that are correct more often than not.

- **Violet**

  Inspirational leaders, performers, visionaries, and teachers tend to have violet-colored auras. Early on in their lives, they will have already felt the need to educate others and lead them towards higher ideals in life. Their ultimate goal is to save the world and inspire others to further improve their own lives.

- **Indigo**

  People who possess indigo auras are said to embody a new type of energy that flows as a result of the current age of relative peace and harmony. Unlike those with violet auras, these individuals do not feel the need to save the world anymore. Instead, they want to set themselves up as role models for others to emulate and follow instead.

- **Lavender**

Spiritually sensitive people exhibit lavender auras. They often have trouble dealing with the realities of life, so they have a habit of withdrawing themselves back into their own little worlds. These people, however, are inclined to surround themselves with objects that are related to magic and supernatural beings, both of which they find to be enchanting and comforting.

- **Magenta**

There are only a few people observed to possess a magenta aura, which incidentally correlates with the color's meaning since this denotes that the person does not conform to standards. They are usually the creative types who prefer to march to the beat of their own drums. They perceive things in a different light, though not necessarily in a supernatural way. These people prefer working with actual, tangible objects that they can alter in some way to make the resulting creation their own.

- **Crystal**

Another rarity among the life colors is the crystal aura. People with such energy are surrounded by a clear inner layer, which earn them the nickname "aura chameleons." Since their auras do not have a color of their own, they end up matching the ones possessed by the people who they are with at any given time. They also tend to adapt the quirks, feelings, and thoughts of whichever color they are associating with. Hence, this makes them excellent companions for any type of personality.

- **Tan**

There are various types of tan aura that denote different meanings. More often than not, they are combined with other life colors, thereby giving the person possessing a tan aura some of the traits shown by other people with different types of auras.

  - **Light Tan**

    Light tan auras signify that those individuals are analytical and methodical in almost all aspects of their lives. Unlike other types of auras, their inner layers are drawn closer towards their bodies, which illustrates how reserved these people can be. They are wary of other people in terms of their physical security and emotional distance. Sharing their thoughts and feelings with others is not something they are comfortable in doing, no matter what situation they are in.

  - **Environmental Tan**

    Tan combined with a layer of forest green color, this type of tan aura is said to be possessed by those who prefer to maintain a balance of the physical and mental aspects in their lives. They explore their surroundings with their senses, but as soon as something piques their interest, they try to analyze immediately what they have stumbled upon.

- **Sensitive Tan**

When combined with a light blue layer, the individual's focus shifts to sustaining a balance of their rationality and emotionality in all aspects of their lives. They also embody some key blue aura traits, such as the need to be in touch with the emotional well-being of other people. Their tan traits, however, are more similar to those of intellectual people who have light tan auras.

- **Abstract Tan**

Of all the tans, people with this type of aura are the most childlike due to the traits that they commonly exhibit. These individuals are known for their congenial approach to others, their open-mindedness, and optimistic outlook in life. Though they are naturally smart and curious, they cannot seem to focus on just one thing at a time. Their attention can be easily pulled in different directions all at once, making them appear scatter-brained sometimes.

How to View and Read Auras

With the technology available today, you do not have to be psychic to see auras. Unfortunately, this form of technology is not readily accessible for most people due to its relatively high cost to operate.

Having a rich spiritual life can assist in the process of aura reading, since reading one's energy requires a profound understanding of the human psyche. You do not need the aid of technology nor an awakened third eye. All you need is to devote some time to practicing the following methods that can develop your skill in seeing and interpreting auras:

1. **Read your own aura**

    One of the hardest but most effective ways of practicing the skill of reading aura is by practicing reading your own. This can pose a challenge since people tend to have preconceived notions about their own personalities and preferences in life. As a result, these biases can influence the outcome of the reading. Still, by choosing to read your own aura first you will not only improve your skills, but also be able to reveal your other latent psychic abilities.

    Start practicing with yourself by sitting down in your preferred meditation spot. If you do not have one yet, look for a place where you relax and be free from any potential distractions.

    Once you are feeling calm and collected, set your objectives by mentally repeating your intent. You may also choose to whisper this under your breath over and over, if you prefer hearing the words.

As you do so, rub your palms together up and down. Continue this motion until you feel a magnetic buildup between your hands.

When you have felt this sensation, concentrate on the area between your palms. If you are successful, you will see a thread of energy emanating from one hand to the other. At the very least, you will feel a sense of which color it is, and you can further infer from that.

However, if you still cannot see anything, then you might need to stop and put this off for another day. Repeat the exercise only when you feel the impulse to make another attempt, since you cannot force yourself to accurately read your own aura.

2. **Practice with your friends**

If you are open about your spirituality and prefer working with other people, then the best method for you to practice may be reading the aura of a friend. It is imperative, however, to seek their permission first before doing so. Auras reveal a lot of personal information that they might not be willing to divulge with you. This means that getting their consent before doing this exercise is the right way to start.

When they have agreed with your request, invite your friends into a quiet place where you can both pay attention without being bothered by other unnecessary stimuli.

Ask them to stand with their backs against a wall that is painted with neutral colors, preferably white. You, on the other hand, should stand in front of them while maintaining a distance of at least 15 inches or 38 centimeters between you and your friends.

After a few minutes of complete silence, inspect the wall, not your friends. While doing so, check if you can sense the energies they are giving off.

From the wall, move your gaze slowly into their bodies before switching back again to the areas of the wall that surrounds their outlines. Ask in a measured voice for the auras to reveal themselves. Wait in silence for any changes and pay attention to any possible shifts in the colors you are currently seeing.

A way of knowing if you are successful or not is by asking your friends to move their arms and bodies slowly. If the colors follow their movements, then you are seeing their actual auras. If not, then you can try to start the process all over again.

Another way of checking your success is by playing upbeat, funky music. If the color in the outer layers of their auras begins to change, then you have succeeded in seeing your friends' auras.

3. **Assess how other people's presence makes you feel**

The easiest way to practice seeing auras is by trying to sense the energies that other people exude. This does not have to be a thorough reading of their whole life, but rather just a feeling of what energy they are currently exuding.

Just take note of how the other person makes you feel whenever he or she is around you. Do you get a gut reaction or a specific physical sensation from being around them? Do they make you feel nervous or excited? Do they inspire you just by merely staying close?

When you have determined how you feel, envision which life color you would associate with that person. Which of the life colors would best describe the type of energy they are giving off? As you get to know the person better, you will gradually learn how accurate your reading is. With continued practice, you will also learn how to easily identify the color of the auras surrounding the people around you.

4. **Develop your peripheral vision**

According to scientific studies, the outside corners of our eyes have more photosensitive cells compared to the inner and middle portions of the eyes. This means that the outer sides have a greater capacity of seeing things that would otherwise be invisible to normal human sight. As such, a well-developed peripheral vision can be a valuable trait in seeing life colors and reading other people's auras.

The main challenge that this method poses is that we are not used to directly utilizing our peripheral vision. Humans are not predisposed to rely on the corner of their eyes, so the muscles involved can get strained after some time.

To overcome this limitation, you can start by exercising these muscles in small increments regularly. Fix your eyes on one spot in front of you for about 30 seconds. Then, let your gaze soften. Take note of the objects that are positioned outside of your direct line of sight. Try to identify them and visualize how they would look if you were viewing them directly. Then, shift your gaze towards the objects and see if you are correct.

Doing this for an extended amount of time is counterintuitive to your goal of strengthening your peripheral vision. Try practicing for short periods of time so as to not strain your eyes. Maintain slow, even breaths during your practice to avoid becoming overwhelmed and losing focus. Through doing this regularly, you will begin noticing the auras of other people without much effort.

Practicing the art of reading auras is a valuable skill that can be helpful in your day-to day life. By understanding the types of auras carried by the people around us, we can improve our interactions with them, and even have the option of getting to choose which company we should keep.

Scientific Ways of Viewing and Measuring Auras

Due to the discovery of technologies that capture the appearance of auras, this concept is no longer limited only to practitioners of the mystical arts and spiritual activities. Auras are now being studied as a real-life phenomenon, though the interpretations of their probable meaning remain contested among experts from different fields.

From the point of view of scientists, auras are believed to be electromagnetic fields that encircle all types of living being—humans, animals, and even plants. The reason for the presence of auras, however, is yet to be explained since these experts do not fully accept that auras reflect the personality, health, and preferences of an individual.

Instead of referring to the color bands of auras in terms of the layers and life colors, scientific experts refer to the field of energy emitted by a person as an auric egg. The full form of the auric egg can extend up to three feet or 92 centimeters around an individual.

To see and capture the image of an auric egg, one of the most popular methods is through Kirlian photography. Using a plate that features an electric flow of high-frequency currents, the energy fields surrounding a person can be exposed during the development process of the photograph.

The captured image proves the existence of auras, as well as the wide array of colors that different individuals may emit. Through this, experts have gained a new way of analyzing auras, whether from a scientific or spiritual perspective.

Chapter 7 – Communicating with Spirit Guides

Before we are born into this world, there are non-corporeal entities that are assigned to us by our higher selves. They are called spirit guides, and their primary aim is to essentially guide us in different ways throughout our lives. These spirit guides are also responsible for advising us on how to fulfill the contractual obligations we have made with our higher selves before coming into being again as our current incarnations.

Some spirit guides are permanent companions, while others remain hidden except during critical moments in your life wherein you are close to achieving your goals, or you are in danger of losing out on the opportunity to attain said goals. There is also no standard level of consciousness for these entities. They can be highly enlightened spirits on par with saints and divine beings. Most, however, are masters only in specific fields of interest.

They can also be gendered, but your personal gender does not dictate whether you will have a masculine or feminine spirit guide. However, this does not mean that they conform to gender roles or expectations. Rather, the energies they emit suggest which gender they closely resemble instead.

Some spirits have former incarnations, but due to certain circumstances in life, they have chosen instead to remain as forms of guiding energy instead. Others, conversely, have never taken physical form.

In some cases, a spirit guide will be assigned only to you. However, the majority of these spirits prefer to guide more than one being at a time, meaning that you share the same spirit guide with other people as well.

In rare cases, people may have deceased family members or loved ones as their spirit guides. But regardless of their origin and form, the main function of the spirit guide remains the same.

How Spirit Guides Help Us

Spirit guides keep watch over their respective human, day in and day out. During certain points in life, they shall make their presence known and intervene in order to influence the decisions and actions of a given individual. According to parapsychologists, spirit guides have various methods of accomplishing such tasks:

- **Through signals**

  Spirit guides can send a message to you through the use of signs. Typically, these signs appear over and over again, until you finally pay attention to the significance of their meaning.

  This can be as simple as a particular scene in a TV show which you keep seeing. You may first see the scene upon your initial viewing, then while passing by someone else who is watching the same TV show, and finally when it got replayed again on the show's advertisement.

When such an instance happens to you, look closer into the meaning behind the scene and determine if this has any significance in your actual life. More often than not, these repeated viewings of the same scene are a message from your spirit guide.

- **Through intuition**

Spirit guides have a penchant for catching your attention through your gut feelings. As such, the expression "follow your gut" can pertain to the moments in your life when these entities try to show you how good or bad your idea is.

Have you ever felt suddenly that something horrible is about to happen, without any explanation or apparent cause for it? This might be your spirit guide warning you of an upcoming disaster that could directly affect you.

- **Through other people in your life**

Spirit guides may also seek the help of other guides in order to get a message sent to you. When they collaborate, they might get their charges to meet up and relay the messages they want to convey.

For instance, one day you find yourself thinking about an old classmate from high school that you have not seen for a long time. Later that day, you see them shopping around the local supermarket. You would probably think that this is a mere coincidence, but more often not, the meeting is actually pre-arranged by your former classmate's guide and your own spirit guide.

Another example is when you are thinking of moving into a new place. If your spirit guide agrees with your plan, then they may set up a "chance" meeting with your realtor the next time you head out to walk in the park.

- **Through manipulation**

There are some spirit guides who can manipulate physical objects in order to nudge you in the right direction. They do this not out of a malevolent intent to harm you, but rather out of a desperate need to get you to pay attention to their cues. After all, humans still have their free will, and subtle attempts to communicate with us may be entirely lost along the way, or totally ignored when noticed.

To illustrate this, picture this common scene wherein you are in a rush to leave the house, but for some reason, you cannot seem to find your car keys. You might be tempted to take the bus instead, but at the last minute the telephone rings. It turns out that it is an important phone call that you would have missed if you had left just a minute earlier.

The most likely culprit who hid away your keys is your spirit guides. They have exhausted all their options, and the only way to get through to you is by literally inconveniencing you. This may be frustrating at times, but these spirit guides know things beyond our understanding, so it is advisable to listen well to what they have to say.

How to Communicate with Your Spirit Guides

Some people do not need to be nudged in the right direction, or manipulated into making a decision that they would not otherwise make. These people have developed their senses to the point where they can actively communicate with the respective spirit guides through sight, hearing, or even touch. To achieve this level of relationship with your spirit guide, there are various ways of increasing your connection that you may consider applying to your daily routine:

- **Practice meditation**

   As with any activity that involves your spiritual life, meditation is the key to establishing healthy communication with your spirit guides. If you have not yet meditated before, then here are some basic instructions that you can follow.

   First, find a quiet place where you can relax away from the typical distractions of life. Breathe in and out slowly. Think of your objective for that session, which is opening a line of communication with your spirit guide. Invite your guide to sit beside you and have a chat. You don't need to have specific questions in mind yet. Just try to get them to accept your request first before delving into deeper matters.

When you are almost in a trance-like state, you will feel the presence of your spirit guide. At first, it will likely be a very subtle experience. But over time and through repeated meditation, you can strengthen this connection until you are finally able to receive key information that would be helpful and applicable to your current situation in life.

- **Dream**

Perhaps one of the easiest ways of creating a direct connection with your spirit guide is through dreams. When we dream, humans are able to meet their guide halfway through our respective dimensions. The downside to this method is that it can be hard to control since it takes a high level of psychic ability to exert control over the direction of our dreams.

There are ways, however, to increase the likelihood of success when using your dreams as a communication channel between you and your spirit guide. The most effective way is to put out your intention to meet with your spirit guide before going to sleep. Think also of the agenda of your meeting, so that you can relate the meaning of your dreams to these when you wake up. There is no guarantee that it will work during your first few tries, but eventually, you will see the effects of consistently asking for a meeting in your dreams.

People who have mastered the art of lucid dreaming can utilize this method effortlessly. Once they have entered their dreams, lucid dreamers can simply request for their spirit guides to appear and then proceed to asking them questions.

- **Keep a journal**

Many psychic experts recommend this method since it is an excellent way of keeping track of your "conversations" with your spirit guides. To start, get yourself a journal. Alternatively, you can choose to type on your computer.

Once you have selected your preferred method, write down any question you have for your spirit guide. Then, keep quiet, and try entering a meditative state of mind. As soon as you hear some semblance of an answer, write down or type the response as you continue to listen on.

At first, it may seem like you are just imagining a conversation with another person. However, do not let this thought stop you. When you reach an answer that does not seem like something that you would say, then pay more attention since the spirit guide is becoming more attuned with your conversation.

As mentioned earlier, the great advantage of using this method is that you get to keep a record of what your spirit guide has said to you. You may refer back to these writings whenever you need advice, or whenever you feel like communicating with them again.

It should be noted that a direct line to your spirit guide cannot be established in an instant. This will require time and regular practice from you. However, the benefits do make the extra effort worth your while.

If none of these methods have worked for you, then you may consider asking for the help of a psychic. Through readings, psychics can identify some—if not all—of your spirit guides. Once a connection has been established, you can then course your queries through the psychic, who shall serve as bridge between you and your spirit guides.

Chapter 8 – Opening and Healing the Chakras

Chakras are specific areas in the human body where fundamental types of energies are received, processed, utilized, and transmitted. The flow of energy from each chakra to the next affects not only our spiritual wellness, but also our physical and emotional health.

Originating from the Sanskrit word for "cyclone", chakras are believed to spinning centers of energy. They may be experienced in various ways by different people. Some describe them in terms of colors; others as flowers that bloom inside of them when the chakras become activated.

Seven Primary Types of Chakras

Each chakra has a specific function and unique focus. Each chakra influences the types of psychic abilities an individual might possess, as well as the rate of development of such gifts, if the said individual wishes to improve upon them.

- **The Root Chakra: Survival**

  The location of the first chakra varies depending on the person's gender. For men, this is located at the base of their spines; among women, between their ovaries.

  It is associated with survival and serves as a constant reminder of our need for physical security. Even if a person does not feel threatened, the energies from this chakra prompt us to look for ways to survive and achieve a sense of stability.

Activating this chakra is necessary for grounding yourself to the planet, which is a vital step in realizing both your conscious and unconscious hopes and desires in life. By being aligned with the frequency of the Earth, you may begin harnessing the planet's energies and use them for your own endeavors.

- **The Sacral Chakra: Boundaries**

Three fingers below the navel is the approximate location of the second chakra. It is believed to lie directly on the pubic bone, which makes it the center for our sexual energies as well. It is important to note, however, that even though the second chakra is linked with the pleasurable aspects of our being, its primary function is focused on assigning our psychic boundaries from other people.

According to parapsychologists, many budding psychics experience troubles with controlling the second chakra. Since people naturally receive the energies emitted by other people in this chakra, inexperienced psychics tend to rely on these unfiltered energies to perform their readings. The problem begins when the energy of other people gets mixed up with the person's own energy. The psychic boundaries become blurred, and the psychic can no longer separate himself from the other person.

As such, experts suggest avoiding the use of this chakra when relating with other people. Bringing other people's energy into your own without knowing how to control it can be emotionally unhealthy for both you and the people around you in the long run. To respect and honor the psychic boundaries that exist between you and the rest of the world, aim to master self-restraint through regular meditation.

- **The Solar Plexus Chakra: Ego**

Just below the point where the ribs come together is the solar plexus, which houses the third chakra. Similar to the human heart—which regulates the circulation of blood throughout the different body systems—the third chakra serves as pump for the psychic energy that flows through your energy centers.

This chakra is also known as the ego chakra since it reflects how well you know yourself. When at its best, the third chakra also allows you to refine your understanding of other people as well.

Since we often use this chakra—whether it is done knowingly or not—many people end up abusing this energy center. This happens when they try to take too much control over their lives due to a misunderstanding of how ego and power works in spiritual terms. Everybody is expected to have an ego, but with maturity, people can learn to let go of their need to control themselves and others in order to fulfill their basic needs, such as survival and social support.

Utilizing the third chakra well means that you are content with gaining an understanding of yourself and others. As a result, you can focus instead on your personal development, and later on seek out ways to collaborate with other people in a healthy way.

- **The Heart Chakra: Love**

Known as the chakra of love, the fourth chakra is located in the middle of the chest. Experts believe that this is where the human spirit connects with the physical body. It controls how well we relate with the community we belong to, as well as the quality of relationships we maintain with the people around us.

The fourth chakra can only work well if the first three chakras are functioning properly. This means that it relies on people's level of maturity since this will serve as a strong foundation of their relationships with the rest of the world.

- **The Throat Chakra: Communication**

The fifth chakra is situated near the base of the neck, and it channels subtle sounds and vibrations that can affect the person's psychic abilities, particularly telepathy. By activating this chakra, a person can open up new ways of communication, as well as further improve their current methods of relaying messages to other people.

The creativity required for proper self-expression originates from the energies transmitted from this chakra. Through this, you can access the freedom to explore your inner mind and create an identity that you will then project to the rest of the world.

- **The Third Eye Chakra: Visualization**

There is complex system of energy centers in the human head, but the core can be found near the pituitary gland that lies around two inches or five centimeters behind the middle of the eyebrows. Because of this, people associate the sixth chakra with the concept of the third eye, which is said to play a vital role in a person's spiritual development.

Parapsychologists also believe that the energies channeled through the sixth chakra promote the development of our psychic sight, or more commonly known as clairvoyance. Visualizations occur when we tap into the sixth chakra, allowing us to "see" visions of scenes and symbols that could be further interpreted as answers rooted in our intuition.

- **The Crown Chakra: Wisdom**

The seventh chakra is located at the top of the head, which explains its most commonly used name - the crown chakra. This is where the culmination of every energy cycle takes place. Activating this chakra allows us to understand our experiences in a comprehensive manner.

Given this, the seventh chakra is associated with wisdom gained through experience and knowledge. Harnessing its energy lets us find meaning from our perceptions of other all living beings and non-living things. This, in turn, ultimately influences our default mode of interaction with the world.

There are two lesser known systems of chakras in our body, aside from the seven that are linked to our nervous system. The chakras located in the arches of the feet open up our body and spirit in order to receive the energy emitted by the planet. Back in the early days of meditation, a practitioner was required to sit down in a lotus position - the most common pose of Buddha figurines sold nowadays. However, with the advent of the Aquarian Age, the foot chakras have again risen to prominence due to their capacity to harness the powers of the Earth. As a result, humans are now able to be one with the world while traveling around to further develop their psychic abilities.

Another lesser known group of chakras are those found in the hands. These are the swirling discs of energies located in each palm. Activating these chakras promotes the healing powers that a spiritual person might possess.

Channeling the energies from the chakras is fundamental for the development of psychic abilities. However, regular usage requires also a consistent cleaning schedule to prevent any blockage in the chakras. This will ensure that you are always at the optimal condition to practice your abilities and further enrich your spiritual life.

Healing Your Chakras

The primary goal of this activity is for you to balance out the different aspects of your life—physical, mental, emotional, and spiritual—with the universal forces that influence your psychic abilities. The following techniques are highly recommended for those who want to clean their chakras:

- **Meditation**

  First and foremost, meditation has been proven to be an effective way of removing blockages and re-establishing the flow of energy into the chakras. There are two approaches to chakra meditation that you may like to consider:

  a. Address the cause of the blockage.

  You start this form of meditation by first identifying the root-cause of your current problems. This should be the initial goal of your meditations since you need to have full awareness of your issues before you can ever hope to solve them.

  Once identified, you can take it a step further by analyzing the causes for possible solutions. At this point, there is no right or wrong answer. All you need to focus on is the fact that you know what your problems is, and that there are ways to solve it.

As you continue to meditate, the right answers will come to you, and your intuition shall immediately recognize their significance. It is now up to you how you will act to fully resolve your issues.

Since you have gone to the root of the problem, the likelihood of its recurrence is low. From here on, you will start experiencing improvements in your energy centers, which will thereby allow you to refocus your efforts in developing your psychic abilities.

b. Alleviate yourself from the effects of the blockage.

Instead of going after the cause, the main objective of this type of meditation is to eliminate or lessen the impact of the effects of a blocked chakra on your physical, mental, emotional, and spiritual well-being. Typically, the effects stem from being isolated from the energies that originate from the planet and even the universe.

There are several methods for achieving this objective. You may try practicing the Inner Vision Meditation, the Wellbeing Boat approach, or the White Light Chakra Meditation, among others. However, if you are not well-versed with such advanced techniques, you can always start with basic meditation routines.

By alleviating the negative effects of the blockage, you can better move on to actually addressing the main cause of the blockage. As a result, you can expect improvements to occur at a quicker rate since you have lightened the burden first.

- **Affirmations**

Affirmations can help heal your chakras since they serve as positive reminders to ourselves. These statements can encourage you to keep your focus on the important matters. They can also be used to wipe away your doubts about your abilities as a psychic being.

There are different affirmations for each type of chakra, since each energy center has a unique purpose and characteristics. Here is a list of examples that you can use as a pattern for your personal affirmations:

- o The First Chakra: "Humility is my virtue. I am content with what I have."

- o The Second Chakra: "I live for my passions. I am strong and radiant."

- o The Third Chakra: "I accept my strengths and weaknesses. There is nothing else I want to change about myself."

- o The Fourth Chakra: "I love unconditionally. Love is always the answer."

- o The Fifth Chakra: "I only speak the truth. My thoughts are always positive and accepting."

- o The Sixth Chakra: "I understand how each one of us is connected. I welcome life's many challenges."

- o The Seventh Chakra: "I am a complete being. I am one with the universe."

- **Massage**

Depending on the specific chakra that you want to work on, a healing massage can be done to clear out the blockages and restore the natural flow of energy to your chakras:

- o The First Chakra

  Focus on the gluteus region down to your legs and feet in order to promote the flow of energy back to these parts of your body.

- o The Second Chakra

  To relieve the tension in your hips and open up the sacral chakra again, you have to focus on hip flexors where you can attain myofascial and iliopsoas muscle release.

o   The Third Chakra

Applying oils while massaging your navel can encourage the elimination of waste, and improve the functioning of nearby bodily organs.

o   The Fourth Chakra

Start your massage at the upper portion of your back, then move along using gentle movements towards the area where your shoulder meets your arm. When the myofascial release occurs in your pectoral muscles, you will feel a soothing sensation that indicates the reopening of this chakra.

o   The Fifth Chakra

To heal the throat chakra, you have to massage gentle the tissues in front and in the back of your neck. You can also focus on the base of your head during this massage.

o   The Sixth Chakra

Brow stripping, a massage technique that involves the upper areas of your face, can be used to clean the third eye chakra. This involves putting pressure on the muscles near your sinuses, temples, and down to the jaw area.

o The Seventh Chakra

A scalp massage is a great way to open up the crown chakra. Pulling the hair and extending the massage down to the neck are also helpful to release more tension in the cranial region.

- **Color Vibration**

Even psychologists agree that the colors around us significantly affect our emotions, general moods, and even physical state. To rebalance the chakras using color, you can try consuming foods that bear the same color as the ones associated with the chakra that needs to be cleaned. You can also opt to change the color of the clothes and accessories you wear. Some even choose to change the color of the lenses in their eyeglasses, just so they can alter the colors they are absorbing through the eyes.

For your reference, here are the colors that represent the different chakras:

o Red – Root Chakra

o Orange – Sacral Chakra

o Yellow – Solar Plexus Chakra

o Green – Heart Chakra

o Blue – Throat Chakra

o Violet – Third Eye Chakra

o   Indigo – Crown Chakra

Our lives can be much more rewarding if we are able to maintain a deep connection with the world, our innate psychic abilities, and optimal perceptive capabilities. By following the techniques in cleaning, and restoring the ideal state of your chakras, you can continually improve upon your given gifts and maximize the benefits that you receive from them.

Chapter 9 – Understanding the Differences Between Telepathy and Telekinesis

Perhaps the two of the most commonly depicted psychic abilities in fiction are telepathy and telekinesis. Since certain characters are typically portrayed to have both of these powers, there is a persistent confusion about the differences between the two among those who are familiar with the non-physical elements of this world.

It does not help as well that films and TV shows tend to exaggerate the manifestations of these psychic abilities. Such instances have caused many people to dismiss telepathy and telekinesis as forms of pseudo-science, and in some cases, those who do possess these skills have developed incorrect assumptions as to how their abilities should look, and what they should be able to do with them.

If you are determined to develop your psychic abilities, then it is important for you to understand how telepathy differs from telekinesis. This will allow you to check if you possess both of these abilities. Recognition, after all, is the first step in developing your psychic abilities.

What Is Telepathy?

The special ability to transmit messages, emotions, and images to another person's mind is called telepathy. It originated from the Greek words "tele" and "patheia", which mean "far away" and "feeling" respectively. Experts describe this as the psychic ability that allows thoughts and feelings to be sent and received through extrasensory means. In the most basic sense, telepathy is manifesting when you know how someone else is feeling without asking them, or looking for overt signs indicating their emotions.

Telepathy is manifesting itself as well when the phone rings, and somehow you know who is on the other end of line, without even needing to check caller ID. Telepathy can also explain the supernatural links that sometimes exist between mothers and their children, as well as between identical twins.

Telepathy exists between humans because everyone is born with psychic abilities. We are also natural empaths, and as such are connected to one another in ways that cannot be fully described by science as we know it today. Following this theory, it is said that there is a collective unconscious, wherein all human experiences and energies accumulate and become as one. Proponents of this theory further suggest that human brains act as antennas which can pick up and send signals to one another. Such an ability allows humans to take part in a phenomenon called the global synchronicity - or special points in time where a majority of the people living on earth are feeling or thinking the same thing without any apparent leader or coordinator.

Since everyone is telepathic, anybody can develop this psychic skill further. However, society has taught us to ignore the things that cannot be fully explained or understood. To overcome this, we should learn to trust and follow our instincts so that we can harness this special ability in our daily lives.

How to Develop Telepathy

If you wish to develop your telepathic abilities, there are some important points that you have to keep in mind. First, in order to develop this skill, focus on applying your abilities to someone with whom you have a close relationship, such as your parents, your spouse, your children, or your close friends. Seek their permission first, however, before beginning any form of psychic exercises with them. Telepathy can give you access to their private thoughts and emotions, so consent is not only vital, but also necessary for the success of your psychic endeavors.

Once you have found a partner to do your training with, you can now start the process of improving your control over your telepathic abilities:

1. **Meditate with your partner**

   Before starting your meditation session, you must learn first how to block out signals coming from your physical senses. You do not need your sense of sight, sound, taste, smell, or touch in order to send and receive psychic information. In fact, these senses can even disrupt the natural flow of energy into your chakras, as well as interrupt your focus that should be allocated to the task at hand.

   To tune out your senses, you can try wearing headphones to play white noise. Blackout goggles are also excellent for eliminating the temptation to use your vision while doing your telepathic exercises. Basically, any tools that will facilitate sensory deprivation are acceptable for this step in the process. Your partner should also block out their senses, so that both of you can fully concentrate on the telepathic messages that will be sent back and forth between the two of you.

When you have learned how to block any input from physical sensations, you must also prepare your body in order for you to reach a relaxed state during meditation. Yoga is an excellent way of achieving this, in addition to various stretching exercises.

If you do yoga or stretching, concentrate on your back, arms, and legs. Remember to take a deep breath whenever you move into a new pose. Exhale slowly only when you are in position. Continue holding your pose for at least 15 seconds before moving on to the next one. When doing so, focus on the feelings of tension leaving your body.

Meditation should be conducted in a place where you can achieve an optimal physical and mental state. Try wearing loosely fitted clothes so that you can be more relaxed. Proper breathing is also important during this activity. Clear out any unwanted thoughts as you exhale so that you can focus on your intention for that session.

Meditating with a partner can be hard at first, but once both you and your partner have grown accustomed to this practice, you will be able to send and receive telepathic messages more effectively.

2. Send a message to your partner through telepathy

To do this step, you must first visualize your partner. Keep your eyes closed as you picture the recipient inside your mind. Imagine how they are positioned next to you. Focus on the details as well—the color of their hair, eyes, how long their hair is, their figure, among other details.

The recipient must also visualize you in the same manner, and at the same time. This will help facilitate the smooth transmittance of messages from one person to the other.

After you have visualized the other person to the maximum of your abilities, recall the times you have personally interacted with this person. How did you feel when you were talking to your partner face-to-face? Were you happy to be in their presence? Or do you have insecurities about them that make you feel anxious whenever they are nearby. Concentrate on these feelings as you try to make a psychic connection with your partner.

When you are first trying out telepathic exercises, it is better to stick to simple words only - something that both you and your partner know. For instance, you have chosen the word "apple" as the content of your telepathic message. Picture that apple inside your head. Visualize the fruit and try to incorporate as much detail as you can - its color, taste, and aroma, for example. Focus your entire mind on the apple. Imagine you are biting into it. Is it sweet? Is it juicy? Include such details into your visualizations.

When your message has finally taken its full shape, you can now proceed to transmitting it to the intended recipient. Imagine that you are describing the apple to the other person. Say in your mind the word "apple" over and over. Then, visualize how the recipient will react once they have understood what you are trying to say.

You should not strain yourself while doing this. There is a difference between exerting your full concentration and forcing yourself too hard. Doing the latter will be counterintuitive since you have to maintain your relaxed state of mind while engaging in this activity.

Once you have imagined a successful transmission of the message, picture the apple being released from your mind. Stop thinking about it. You have already given it to the other person.

The recipient must remain in their relaxed state during the entirety of your transmission. They should only open their eyes when they have sensed the arrival of the message in their mind. Upon such an event, they must write down whatever information they have received. Tell them to write as much detail as they can, in addition to the word itself.

In order to obtain objective and unquestionable results, it is recommended for you to write down the word you have sent, as well as the descriptions of the object that you visualized. By doing this, neither of you will be able to deny the authenticity of the telepathic transmission that has just happened. It will also show you how well you have done during the visualization portion of this exercise.

When both you and your partner are ready, compare the words you have written. See if the word and object you have sent out has been received accurately by your partner. If you do not match up at all, or if there are certain details that did not get transmitted properly, do not feel discouraged since this is expected for beginners. Take a well-deserved rest before starting the process again.

Aside from sending messages to your partner through telepathic means, there are several other ways to train your psychic abilities. Taking turns in receiving and sending messages can make this activity less tedious and more exciting for the both of you.

Another method is by using Zener cards or a set of five cards with unique symbols featured on each. Place the cards in a downward position between you and your partner. Tell the other person to pick a card from the set. Once he has selected his card, instruct him to look into the symbol intently. As he does this, try to sense what the image is by looking at the card through his mind. When you are ready, share your answer, and see if you are correct.

You can also switch roles for this exercise. When you have selected the card, try to transmit the image via telepathy to your partner. You will know if you are successful when their guess matches with the card in your hand.

Similarly, drawing images can also be a way to transmit telepathic messages to your partner. Once you have drawn an image, visualize the act of sending the details of your drawing to your partner. When they have received your message, tell them to draw the image that has appeared in their mind. Again, the roles for this exercise can be switched up. Your partner will draw an image, while you try to figure out what they have drawn by tapping into their mind.

Regardless of the method you choose, it is highly recommended for you to document your progress in a journal. Record both your successful and failed attempts as a reference for future use. Take note of the words and images that you have transmitted correctly, and which ones could be improved upon further. Be as detailed as possible so that your journal will be useful later on.

What Is Telekinesis?

Psychokinesis—or telekinesis, as it is more commonly known—refers to the ability to move objects with just the power of the mind. Manifestations of this psychic ability can be on a macro level, wherein the person can move large objects or influence the movement of smoke so that it will head in a specific direction. Conversely, this ability can manifest in small ways that are not readily visible to the naked eye, such as influencing the outcome of a thrown dice.

Experts believe that individuals who possess telekinesis are surrounded by a thicker layer of electromagnctic field, especially around the head. Furthermore, they believe that this is the primary source of energy of these psychics, allowing them to perform certain acts of telekinesis. This means that the higher the level of electromagnetism observed around a person, the stronger the telekinetic abilities are.

There are various sub-types of telekinesis that have been exhibited by famous psychics over the years. A person can possess more than one of these skills, along with other psychic abilities.

- **Aerokinesis**

  People who have this ability can control how strong a gust of wind can be. Some psychics can even alter the direction of the wind.

- **Biokinesis**

  Spontaneous healing of injuries gained through accidents and other physical trauma is said to be a manifestation of biokinesis. Basically, these people can influence how fast and how effective their bodies are at self-healing.

- **Cryokinesis**

  Psychics possessing this sub-type of telekinesis hold power over ice. They can make frost appear out of nowhere, and even influence how strong a snowstorm will be.

- **Electrokinesis**

  This refers to the ability to influence or affect electronic equipment. In some cases, the mere presence of a person possessing this skill can cause nearby electronic devices to malfunction. Others report that these psychics are capable of switching the channels on a television with just their mind.

* **Hydrokinesis**

Possessing this ability allows the person to change how water molecules behave. This can be manifested in various ways. Some can alter the water temperature, going from hot to cold and vice versa. Others are said to be able to change the direction and speed of water flow.

The psychic exercise called "cloud bursting" applies mainly to hydrokinetic people. This activity involves gazing up at the sky and focusing on the clouds. With intense concentration, a psychic can change the shape of the clouds, or even form new clouds.

* **Pyrokinesis**

When you are able to cause fire or change the intensity of a flame with just your mind, then you have pyrokinetic abilities.

How to Develop Telekinesis

Unlike other forms of psychic abilities, there is little evidence that telekinesis is real. Skeptics require proof that can be measured and tested, but people who claim to have telekinetic powers have not been able to provide consistent enough results to be considered as valid evidence. As such, there are many people who believe this to be only a product of an overactive imagination.

Even though telekinesis remains to be controversial topic even among parapsychologists, there are people who still believe that this psychic ability is real, and therefore can be trained to its full potential. If you are one of those individuals, then here is list of methods that you can do yourself in order to activate and develop your telekinetic powers:

1. **Meditate**

Before incorporating meditation into your telekinetic exercises, you have to believe first in the concept of telekinesis, and the fact that you do possess this ability, whether or not you have any hard evidence. If deep down, you do not believe that telekinesis is real, then you will not be able to tap into this psychic ability at all. So, the first task that you should undertake is to ensure your 100% confidence in pursuing your quest towards mastering telekinesis.

Read materials about telekinesis. Watch documentaries about the special feats done by famous psychics throughout the years. To feel inspired, you can research more about the life and abilities of Uri Geller, who is perhaps one of the most famous telekinetic performers in modern times. He is known for his exhibitions in front of a live audience, which have featured different types of telekinetic acts, including bending a spoon with his mind. He has claimed that such powers were bestowed upon him by extraterrestrial life forms, but there is no proof of such an incident actually happening to him. If you have managed to increase your level of belief in telekinesis by the end of your research, then you are ready for the next steps in your journey.

By having a total belief in telekinesis and your capacity for it, you can expect to have a deeper level of understanding about what you are trying to do. Furthermore, you will be able to concentrate more on the exercises since you will have eliminated any and all doubts that may have been plaguing your mind.

Attaining this state of mind can help you achieve a relaxed state of being, which is necessary for having a successful meditation session. You may also try taking a nice, long, hot bath before meditating to further relax your body and mind.

When you are ready, look for a quiet spot where you can focus entirely on meditating. During your meditation, think of an object that you could describe with a high level of detail even with your eyes closed. For example, let's assume you have selected a simple, white teacup.

The next step requires your full concentration - but avoid forcing yourself. While keeping the image of the teacup in your mind, visualize how you would like to move this object. Do you want to move it an inch to its right? Or do you want to give it a little shake? Again, you have to get yourself to imagine the tiniest details of your intended act.

You do not have to actually move any object while you are meditating. The point of this activity is simply to get your mind on the right track. You have to be patient with the rate of your development because telekinesis is not something that you can develop in just one or two tries.

To improve the rate of your training, however, you have to include meditation into your daily routine. Make sure that you can meditate for at least 15 minutes per day. In addition, avoid comparing yourself with other people who are doing the same thing as you. Everybody progresses differently, depending on their innate skills, level of dedication, and motivation. If you do remain patient and consistent with your training, then you will eventually see an improvement in your telepathic skills.

2. Practice using telekinetic exercises

Aside from meditation, parapsychologists recommend certain psychic exercises that can be done to demonstrate the level of telekinetic abilities that a person have. You can, however, use meditation as a form of warmup before doing these exercises in order to first achieve the right state of mind.

Some people use the Psi-ball approach, which involves warming up your hands by rubbing them together for about 1 to 2 minutes. This will then activate the electromagnetic fields surrounding your hands, which are essential for telekinesis. After rubbing your hands, pull them apart slightly, and check if you can feel a ball of energy forming in between your palms. Try to play with it to get a better sense of the energy you have generated. Doing this warmup regularly is an excellent way to prepare for conducting the following examples of telekinetic exercises:

a. Bending the flame

Light a candle and place it in front of you. Concentrate on the flame itself, and visualize it moving towards a different direction. Make sure that there is no wind blowing across the candle, so that you can be sure that the movement has been caused by your telekinetic powers.

b. Levitating a feather

Get a feather and a small jar with lid. Place the feather inside the jar, and seal the jar again tightly, ensuring that no air can get inside. Your objective for this exercise is to move the feather from side to side, or better yet, to make the feather float inside the jar.

c. Moving the pen

Put a pen on a flat surface. Sit down in front of the pen and take a deep breath. Visualize the pen rolling towards the right, then towards the left. Concentrate on the object until you can channel your energy into it. The goal is to get the pen moving in the direction that you want.

d. Moving the cork

What you need for this exercise is a bowl of water and a piece of cork – a basic cork found in wine bottles will do fine for this activity. Cork naturally floats in water, but unless there is another outside force pushing or pulling it, the cork should not move at all. Practice moving the floating cork across the surface of the water. Visualize how fast you want it to move, and in which direction it should go. Focus your mental energy toward making the desired movements happen.

e. Swinging a pendulum

If you do not own a pendulum, you can create your own with string and a simple ring without any gemstone embedded in it, or a key, in case you do not have such kind of ring. When you have your pendulum ready, hang it on a hook in front of you. Focus on the pendant portion of the pendulum, and visualize it swinging to and fro. If you are successful in harnessing your telekinetic powers, the pendulum will begin swinging according to how you imagined it. Again, make sure that you are doing this exercise in an area where the wind cannot influence the outcome.

f. Crushing a soda can

For advanced practitioners, a more challenging telekinetic exercise is crushing solid but malleable objects. Therefore, an empty soda can is the perfect choice for this activity. You can start by placing the soda can on a flat surface, keeping it within your arm's reach. Position one hand over the can, but do not touch it. Concentrate on the object as you visualize your energy slowly surrounding the sides of the can, as if you are gripping it with your own hand. When the energy has fully enclosed the can, compress it as tightly as you can without straining yourself. If you have managed to crush the can, or even create a dent on it, then you have achieved success in this exercise.

No matter which of these exercises you choose to try, you have to remember the three basic steps in using your telekinetic powers. Focus your energy. Visualize the movements. Move the object according to your will.

With constant practice and continued devotion to your objectives, you will eventually achieve the results that you are hoping to get.

Conclusion

Thanks again for taking the time to read this book!

You should now have a good understanding of the different psychic abilities, and how they can be developed. I hope you found this book to be helpful, and I wish you the best of luck in your future spiritual endeavors!

If you enjoyed this book, please take the time to leave me a review on Amazon. I appreciate your honest feedback, and it really helps me to continue producing high quality books.

www.ingramcontent.com/pod-product-compliance
Lightning Source LLC
Chambersburg PA
CBHW051543050726
47595CB00002B/618